Unique Design:

connecting with the Christian community

Bible Study That Builds Christian Community

SERENDIPITY
H O U S E

LIFE
CONNECTIONS

ISBN: 1-5749-4066-X

Unless otherwise indicated, all Scripture quotations are from the Holy Bible,
New International Version, copyright © 1973, 1978, 1984
by International Bible Society. Used by permission.

To order additional copies of this resource:
ORDER ONLINE at *www.serendipityhouse.com*;
VISIT the LifeWay Christian Store serving you;
WRITE Serendipity House
117 10th Avenue, North
Nashville, TN 37234
FAX (615) 277-8181
PHONE (800) 525-9563

Printed in the United States of America

117 10th Avenue, North
Nashville, Tennessee 37234

Contents

Core Values

Community: The purpose of this curriculum is to build community within the body of believers around Jesus Christ.

Group Process: To build community, the curriculum must be designed to take a group through a step-by-step process of sharing your story with one another.

Interactive Bible Study: To share your "story," the approach to Scripture in the curriculum needs to be open-ended and right-brained—to "level the playing field" and encourage everyone to share.

Developmental Stages: To provide a healthy program in the life cycle of a group, the curriculum needs to offer courses on three levels of commitment:

(1) Beginner Level—low-level entry, high structure, to level the playing field;
(2) Growth Level—deeper Bible study, flexible structure, to encourage group accountability;
(3) Discipleship Level—in-depth Bible study, open structure, to move the group into high gear.

Target Audiences: To build community throughout the culture of the church, the curriculum needs to be flexible, adaptable, and transferable into the structure of the average church.

Mission: To expand the kingdom of God one person at a time by filling the "empty chair." (We add an extra chair to each group session to remind us of our mission.)

Group Covenant

It is important that your group covenant together, agreeing to live out important group values. Once these values are agreed upon, your group will be on its way to experiencing Christian community. It's very important that your group discuss these values—preferably as you begin this study. The first session would be most appropriate. (Check the rules to which each member of your group agrees.)

- ☐ **Priority:** While you are in this course of study, you give the group meetings priority.
- ☐ **Participation:** Everyone is encouraged to participate and no one dominates.
- ☐ **Respect:** Everyone is given the right to his or her own opinion, and all questions are encouraged and respected.
- ☐ **Confidentiality:** Anything that is said in the meeting is never repeated outside the meeting.
- ☐ **Life Change:** We will regularly assess our own life-change goals and encourage one another in our pursuit of Christlikeness.
- ☐ **Empty Chair:** The group stays open to reaching new people at every meeting.
- ☐ **Care and Support:** Permission is given to call upon each other at any time, especially in times of crisis. The group will provide care for every member.
- ☐ **Accountability:** We agree to let the members of the group hold us accountable to the commitments we make in whatever loving ways we decide upon.
- ☐ **Mission:** We will do everything in our power to start a new group.
- ☐ **Ministry:** The group will encourage one another to volunteer and serve in a ministry and to support missions by giving financially and/or personally serving.

For the Leader

Each group meeting consists of a three-part agenda:

Icebreaker – Fun questions designed to warm the group and build understanding about other group members. These questions prepare the group for meaningful discussion throughout the session.

Bible Study – The heart of each session is the Bible study time. The Life Connections series involves six easy-to-understand segments.

1. **Scripture Reading** – Each Bible study begins with the reading of the focal passage.
2. **About Today's Session** – This section of the Bible Study time is designed to peak the interest of attendees and introduce the theme for the session. In most instances there will be a reminder of what was studied the previous week, a captivating illustration or analogy related to everyday life, and a statement describing what life-changing topic will be given attention.
3. **Identifying with the Story** – During this segment of the Bible Study, subgroups learn more about each other by answering questions that will help them share their story. These questions directly relate to the topic for the day.
4. **Today's Session** – This short teaching time will be led by the Master Teacher. These scripted teachings include a depth of biblical understanding, fascinating illustrations, analogies, statistics, and stories that will spark questions and conviction.
5. **Learning from the Story** – Subgroups will gather to answer a series of questions that anticipate commitment to applying the truths taught.
6. **Life Change Lessons** – The Master Teacher gives practical suggestions that will aid attendees in carrying out the commitments they make.

Caring Time – All study should point us to action. Each session ends with prayer and direction in caring for the needs of group members. Time is also provided to pray for the "empty chair." The empty chair is a visible symbol of the need for each group to lead an unbeliever to a relationship with Jesus Christ.

The cross icon and boxed text represents portions of the student book that have been reprinted in this book.

Every Life Connections group must fill three important roles. Each responsibility is vital to the success of the class.

Teacher – The teacher is the key leader of any Life Connections group. It is the responsibility of the teacher to:

1. enlist facilitators and apprentices.
2. make facilitators and apprentices aware of their roles and be certain these responsibilities are carried out.
3. meet periodically with facilitators to train, encourage, and inspire them.
4. cast vision for and keep the group focused on the goals of the group.
5. guide group members to understand and commit to the group covenant.
6. be sure the group utilizes, fills, and evangelizes through use of the empty chair concept.
7. act as the Master Teacher for the group.
8. keep the group on task throughout each session.

Facilitator – Each subgroup will have a facilitator. It is the responsibility of the facilitators to:

1. lead each individual in their subgroup to participate in Icebreaker activities.
2. involve all members in their subgroup in the Identifying with the Story section of the study.
3. guide those in their subgroup to commit to apply the lessons learned in the Learning from the Story section of the weekly session.
4. with sensitivity and wisdom lead their subgroup to minister to one another during the Caring Time and involve their subgroup in ministry and evangelism.
5. minister to the needs of their subgroup members and lead them to minister to the needs of one another both during and between meetings.

Apprentice – Every subgroup must have an apprentice. When the group consistently has eight or more in attendance, the group should divide into two groups. The apprentice will become the facilitator of the new group and choose an apprentice who will someday be the facilitator of a group. It is the role of the apprentice to:

1. learn from the facilitator of their group.
2. make welcome all new subgroup members.
3. be certain student books and pens or pencils are available for all participants.
4. turn in prayer requests.
5. encourage participation by actively participating themselves.
6. lead the group when the facilitator is unavailable.

For more information and frequently asked questions about Life Connections, visit our Web site at *www.serendipityhouse.com*.

Session

1

Made in the Image of God

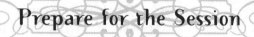

Prepare for the Session

	READINGS	REFLECTIVE QUESTIONS
Monday	Genesis 1:26–27	How do others see God's image in your life?
Tuesday	Genesis 1:28–31	In what specific ways has God blessed you and provided for you?
Wednesday	Psalm 139:13–16	How does it help you to know that all of your days are ordained by God?
Thursday	Ephesians 1:17	What will you do this week to get to know God better?
Friday	Hebrews 10:24–25	How can you encourage someone this week?
Saturday	Psalm 8:5–8	Think about your responsibility as a God-appointed caretaker of His creation. What can you do to fulfill that responsibility?
Sunday	Proverbs 8:30–31	Take some time to rejoice in God's presence.

notes:

🐴 **In groups of 6–8, gather people in a horseshoe configuration.**

Make sure everyone has a name tag.

Take time to share information on class parties that are coming up as well as any relevant church events.

✝ BIBLE STUDY

- to realize that God began designing us for ministry before we were born
- to understand how man and woman were uniquely created to fulfill God's purpose
- to understand that we were created with a need for community

LIFE CHANGE

- to invest time in knowing God more fully by studying the Bible and praying on a regular basis
- to invest time in developing meaningful relationships with other believers by regularly participating in a small group
- to be faithful in fulfilling our God-given responsibilities as adults, spouses, parents, employees, etc.

Icebreaker   (10-15 minutes)

Look-alike! Take turns answering the following questions, going around the group on each question: Has anyone ever told you that you resemble someone famous? If so, who? Do any of your group members resemble someone famous? If so, who? If you could resemble someone famous for a day, who would you want to look like and why?

Men:	Women:
☐ Ricky Martin	☐ Britney Spears
☐ Harrison Ford	☐ Julia Roberts
☐ Denzel Washington	☐ Whitney Houston
☐ Regis Philbin	☐ Halle Berry
☐ Other:_____	☐ Other:_____

INTRODUCE THE ICEBREAKER ACTIVITY: The students have been given instructions in their books.

After the Icebreaker say something like, "It can be fun to see how we resemble other people. But even before we were born, God was designing us to resemble Him. God has created each of us in His image. That is what this session is about."

Hand out the Prayer/Praise Report. A sample copy is on pages 158-159. Have people write down prayer requests and praises. Then have the prayer coordinator collect the report and make copies for use during the Caring Time.

notes:

LEARNING FROM
THE BIBLE

GENESIS 1:26–31

**Have two members
of the class (one
for each passage),
selected ahead of
time, read the
Scripture passages
from Genesis
and Psalms.**

PSALM 139:13–16

Bible Study (30-45 minutes)

The Scripture for this week:

²⁶Then God said, "Let us make man in our image, in our likeness, and let them rule over the fish of the sea and the birds of the air, over the livestock, over all the earth, and over all the creatures that move along the ground."

²⁷So God created man in his own image, in the image of God he created him; male and female he created them.

²⁸God blessed them and said to them, "Be fruitful and increase in number; fill the earth and subdue it. Rule over the fish of the sea and the birds of the air and over every living creature that moves on the ground."

²⁹Then God said, "I give you every seed-bearing plant on the face of the whole earth and every tree that has fruit with seed in it. They will be yours for food. ³⁰And to all the beasts of the earth and all the birds of the air and all the creatures that move on the ground—everything that has the breath of life in it—I give every green plant for food." And it was so.

³¹God saw all that he had made, and it was very good. And there was evening, and there was morning—the sixth day.

¹³For you created my inmost being; you knit me together in my mother's womb.

¹⁴I praise you because I am fearfully and wonderfully made; your works are wonderful, I know that full well.

¹⁵My frame was not hidden from you when I was made in the secret place. When I was woven together in the depths of the earth, ¹⁶your eyes saw my unformed body. All the days ordained for me were written in your book before one of them came to be.

notes:

...about today's session (5 minutes)

MADE WITH PURPOSE

You've probably heard someone refer to a successful person as a "self-made" man or woman. The truth is none of us had a say in being made. We were not born into this world by accident (although your parents may not agree!). Some of the most discouraged people around are those who seem to simply exist, without an awareness of why they're on this earth. They seem to have no direction or meaning in their lives. Sadly, the message is being conveyed to many of our children in the classroom and in the media that they are just a result of natural causes and chemical reactions that began millions of years ago.

We are much more than just a little higher than apes. We are the product of a God who did not create us on a whim. Instead, He put careful thought and His perfect wisdom, wisdom beyond human comprehension, into forming and shaping us. As you look around this room, you'll notice that no one is exactly the same. There is no common mold. Some of us are extroverts, while others are introverts. Some have blonde hair, while others have brown. Some have light skin, while others have darker skin. Some are technical thinkers, while others are abstract thinkers. When God made you, He broke the mold! You are a unique creation of God.

However, God did create us with some similarities. You and I were created in the image of God. We are given the privilege of reflecting God's greatness and goodness to everyone around us. In addition to doing this as God's "lighthouse" in a sin-darkened world, we are to do this within the context of a community of believers, the church.

We will look at the creation of Adam and Eve to discover God's purpose in creating us. We'll also look at Psalm 139 and see God's sovereign involvement in our existence.

notes:

Summarize these introductory remarks. Be sure to include the underlined information, which gives the answers to the student book questions (provided in the margin).

Begin with something like: "This is our first session of *Unique Design: Connecting with the Christian Community.* In this 13-week study we will look at how we are uniquely crafted to serve one another within the body of Christ. God desires to work through His people to accomplish His purposes. Today, we will look at the significance of God creating us in His image."

What message is being conveyed to our children in the classroom and in the media?

What privilege is yours as a child of God?

1

✝

◡ Remain in groups of 6–8 people, in a horseshoe configuration.

In this small-group session, students will be responding to the following questions that will help them share their stories in terms of the story of Adam and Eve's creation as well as David's words in Psalm 139.

Have the students explore these questions together.

Identifying with the Story (5-7 minutes)

1. God gave Adam and Eve specific responsibilities to fulfill. Which of the following areas do you feel is the most difficult responsibility for you to fulfill?

   ☐ employee   ☐ parent
   ☐ spouse   ☐ student
   ☐ church leader   ☐ wise steward
   ☐ law-abiding citizen   ☐ other:_____
   ☐ loyal friend

2. God promised to meet all of Adam and Eve's needs. Suppose you were in their shoes (did they have shoes?) and you were given the chance to ask God for something. Which of the following would you have requested? (Choose only one.)

   ☐ a sport-utility vehicle (Where would you go?)
   ☐ cable TV (What would you watch?)
   ☐ a radio (What would you listen to?)
   ☐ a new wardrobe (Who would be impressed by it?)
   ☐ a million dollars (Where would you spend it?)
   ☐ a computer (Who would you connect to?)
   ☐ sports equipment (Who would you play?)
   ☐ other:_____

3. In Psalm 139, David writes about God's sovereign involvement in creating him and ordaining all the days of his life. What about this passage brings the most comfort and encouragement to your life right now?

   ☐ God planned my coming into this world—I am not an accident of nature.
   ☐ God made me unique, unlike anyone else.
   ☐ God knew all about me before I was born.
   ☐ God knows what I've been through in the past.
   ☐ I'll never go through anything that will surprise God.

notes:

Share with your class the following information which you may modify according to your own perspectives and teaching needs. The answers to the student book questions (provided in the margin) are underlined.

What are three truths associated with being created in the image of God?

today's session (15-20 minutes)

In these two sections of the Bible we see some important truths which help us understand the significance of being created in the image of God. Let's look at three of these truths.

We Were Created with a Need for Community

Community is the network of meaningful relationships believers experience where purpose, encouragement, accountability, fellowship, and life are shared. All of us have a desire to belong. Why do we all seem to have this common desire? Because community is reflected in God's very nature. In Genesis 1:26, we see God using language signifying community—"us" ... "our" ... "our." Hebrew scholars call this the *plural of majesty* also seen in Genesis 11:7 and Isaiah 6:8. This grammatical form shows God's involvement in an activity with all the fullness of His being. Also, consider the Hebrew word for God, "Elohim." This word contains a plural suffix that affirms the New Testament understanding of God as a trinity—Father, Son, and Holy Spirit—one God expressed in three distinct persons in community.

When God created man in His image, God created man and woman with a need for community. In Genesis 2:18, we read that it is not good for man to be alone. So, God created Eve from the rib of Adam. And, most importantly, Adam and Eve were in community with God, enjoying an intimate relationship with Him. In the New Testament, we get a picture of our need for meaningful fellowship by taking a look at several of the "one anothers." Here is a partial list:

"Serve one another"	Galatians 5:13
"Accept one another"	Romans 15:7
"Forgive ... one another"	Colossians 3:13
"Greet one another"	Romans 16:16
"Carry each other's burdens"	Galatians 6:2
"Be devoted to one another"	Romans 12:10
"Honor one another"	Romans 12:10
"Instruct one another"	Romans 15:14
"Submit to one another"	Ephesians 5:21
"Encourage one another"	1 Thessalonians 5:11

We Were Created to Reflect God's Glory

In Numbers 14:21 we learn that the glory of the Lord fills the whole earth. And Habakkuk 2:14 says, "For the earth will be filled with the knowledge of the glory of the Lord, as the waters cover the sea." In Genesis 1:26,28 we read that God gave man and woman the responsibility to subdue the earth and to multiply and fill the earth. Implied here is that we have been given the responsibility to spread God's glory.

today's session (cont'd)

What exactly is the glory of God? We find a clue in Exodus 33:18–19 where Moses asked God to show him His glory. God's response was: " 'I will cause all my goodness to pass in front of you, and I will proclaim my name, the Lord, in your presence.' " In Genesis 1:31, God looked at all He had made and determined, "it was very good." It is logical to conclude that the glory that God intends for each of us to reflect is His goodness and the greatness of His name. In Matthew 5:15, Jesus uses the analogy of a lamp set on a table to describe how we can reflect God's glory in our lives. In Matthew 5:16, Jesus describes the glory and its result: " 'Let your light shine before men, that they may see your good deeds and praise your Father in heaven.' "

We also give God glory when we find our greatest satisfaction in Him. And when we realize there's no substitute for God in our lives, we glorify Him. We make Him glorious and honorable.

In Matthew 22:15–22, we see an interesting interaction between the Pharisees and Jesus. In their attempt to trick Jesus, they asked Him this question: "Is it right to pay taxes to Caesar or not?" (v. 17). Jesus asked to see the coin which had the image of Caesar stamped on it. Jesus then responded with this answer: " 'Give to Caesar what is Caesar's, and to God what is God's' " (v. 21). Basically, Jesus said that the coin was stamped with Caesar's likeness and he had full rights to it. Jesus was also implying that people have the image or likeness of God stamped on them. As the image-bearers of God, we glorify Him by refusing to cling to anything that claims His place in our lives. We glorify God by giving up any idols and giving ourselves to the One whose image is stamped on us. We'll know we've committed our lives completely to God when we acknowledge God's goodness and power in our lives.

We Were Uniquely Designed for God's Purpose

In Genesis 1:26–31, we see that God gave Adam and Eve specific responsibilities. They were created with purpose. As part of that purpose, God gave mankind the intellect and ability to care for God's creation: the earth, its creatures, and the vegetation that produced food. In Psalm 139:13–16, David affirms this truth by describing God's intimate involvement in creating us for His purposes. How involved was God in creating you? Consider these facts concerning the basic makeup of a human:

The largest molecule is called the DNA (deoxyribonucleic acid). The DNA strand carries the hereditary information from the parent to the offspring in all living things. It contains the genetic code and determines whether you will turn out to be a man, mushroom, dandelion or dinosaur. The total length of the DNA strand in one cell is six feet. If all the DNA strands in the body were bunched up they could fit into a box the size of an ice cube. But if unwound and joined together, the string could stretch from the earth to the sun and back more than 400 times.[1]

You are no accident nor just a "higher animal." You were personally designed by God. In Ephesians 2:10, Paul reiterates the truth that God has a plan for each of us: "For we are God's workmanship, created in Christ Jesus to do good works, which God prepared in advance for us to do." Before time began, God planned great opportunities for us as His children to participate in His purposes.

There's a great story from the Old Testament that illustrates this truth. In Genesis, we read of the difficulties Joseph experienced: he was sold as a slave by his own brothers; falsely accused of sexually assaulting Potiphar's wife; imprisoned as an innocent man; and forgotten by the chief cupbearer. Amazingly, all of this was part of God's plan to use Joseph in accomplishing His purposes. After Joseph correctly interpreted Pharaoh's dreams, he was made second-in-charge to Pharaoh. God used Joseph to save the lives of many in Egypt and in Israel including his own family. In addressing his brothers in Genesis 50:20, here's how Joseph described God's purpose for his life: "You intended to harm me, but God intended it for good to accomplish what is now being done, the saving of many lives."

In Genesis 50:20, how did Joseph describe God's purpose for his life?

notes:

⚓ Remain in groups of 6–8 people, in a horseshoe configuration.

In this small-group session, students will be applying the lessons of the text to their own lives through the following questions.

The students were asked (in the student book) to choose an answer for each question and explain why.

Learning from the Story (5-7 minutes)

1. Adam and Eve were dependent on God to meet their most basic needs. List 10 needs that God is meeting in the lives of the members of your group that we often take for granted.

   a. _____

   b. _____

   c. _____

   d. _____

   e. _____

   f. _____

   g. _____

   h. _____

   i. _____

   j. _____

2. Adam and Eve were created to fellowship with God and each other. How does actively participating in fellowship with other believers help you in serving God's purposes? Why do we need each other?

3. Pick a couple of the following areas and list some practical ways you can reflect God's glory through them.

   ☐ raising my children   ☐ working
   ☐ relating with my spouse   ☐ serving at church
   ☐ driving my car   ☐ talking with others
   ☐ playing sports   ☐ other:_____
   ☐ handling my finances

notes:

life change lessons (5-7 minutes)

Share with the class the following thoughts on how the lessons of this text might be applied today. The answers to the student book questions (provided in the margin) are underlined unless the question requires a personal answer.

What are three ways you can reflect God's glory?

a. Invest time in _____.

b. Invest time in _____ with other believers.

As we saw in our groups, we all need encouragement in being image-bearers of God. Here are some ways you can learn to reflect God's glory:

1. INVEST TIME IN KNOWING GOD MORE FULLY. Adam and Eve experienced unhindered, intimate fellowship with God. In Christ, you gained the same privilege as well as the ability to know God in increasing measure. In Ephesians 1:17 Paul writes, "I keep asking that the God of our Lord Jesus Christ, the glorious Father, may give you the Spirit of wisdom and revelation, so that you may know him better." The better you know God and His goodness, the greater your desire to share His goodness with others.

   What you can do: Study God's Word and pray on a regular basis.

2. INVEST TIME IN DEVELOPING MEANINGFUL RELATIONSHIPS WITH OTHER BELIEVERS. God knows it's not good for you to be alone. He knows you need a community of believers. In Hebrews 10:24–25, we are told to spend the time and effort needed to help each other display love and good deeds: "Let us consider how we may spur one another on toward love and good deeds. Let us not give up meeting together, as some are in the habit of doing, but let us encourage one another—and all the more as you see the Day approaching."

   What you can do: Regularly participate in a small-group meeting of fellow believers like this one for the purpose of receiving and giving encouragement with a mutual desire to help each other become better image-bearers of God's glory.

c. Be faithful in _____.

List your top three God-given responsibilities.

3. BE FAITHFUL IN FULFILLING YOUR GOD-GIVEN RESPONSIBILITIES. Like Adam and Eve, God has given each of us different responsibilities. We are to be faithful in fulfilling them for the purpose of exhibiting God's glory and worth. Whether it's fulfilling your role as a parent, spouse, employee, etc., God's desire is that you spread the greatness of His name throughout the earth. What are your top three God-given responsibilities?

   What you can do: Be committed to knowing and carrying out your God-given responsibilities.

notes:

notes:

Caring Time   (15-20 minutes)

This is the time for developing and expressing your caring for group members by praying for each other. Take turns praying for the strength and grace to be faithful in fulfilling your God-given responsibilities. Also, use the Prayer/Praise Report and pray for the concerns listed. If you would like to pray silently, say the word "Amen" when you have finished your prayer so the next person will know when to start.

notes:

⋃ CARING TIME
Remain in groups of 6–8 people, in a horseshoe configuration.

Hand out the Prayer/ Praise Report to the entire group. Ask each subgroup to pray for the empty chair. Pray specifically for God to guide you to someone to bring next week to fill that chair.

After a sufficient time of prayer in subgroups, close in a corporate prayer. Say, "Next week we will talk about: 'My Personality.'"

Ask participants to prepare for next week's session by completing the daily Scripture readings and reflective questions found on page 20.

BIBLE STUDY NOTES

Reference Notes

Use these notes to gain further understanding
of the text as you study on your own.

GENESIS 1:26
God's likeness

image ... likeness. How are we made in the image of God? We were not created exactly like God because we were created with a physical body. However, we do reflect God's character and triune nature (body, soul, and spirit). In doing so, we display God's glory and goodness in the way we think, feel, make choices, and love.

let them rule. Rule as wise stewards of the earth over everything contained on it. God desires that we act in wise and prudent ways to manage all that He has made (see Ps. 8:5–8).

GENESIS 1:27

Man and woman were the crowning act of God's creation. Both bear the stamp of God's image.

GENESIS 1:28
blessing

God blessed them. God was happy with what He had made (see Prov. 8:30–31).

subdue. This term means to "bring into bondage." It is used here in a positive sense. We are charged by God to act as wise managers with the authority to take care of everything God made.

GENESIS 1:29

Some think that before the fall people and animals were vegetarians because there is no mention of eating meat in this passage.

GENESIS 1:31
good work

very good. The term *good* is used here for the seventh time in the creation account (Gen. 1:4,10,12,18,21,25). The earth and all its inhabitants were created to reflect and display the goodness, glory, and worthiness of God.

PSALM 139:13

created my inmost being. David knew that God had created every molecule of his body and the innermost core of who he was—his spirit, conscience, will, and emotions.

PSALM 139:14
wonderfully made

fearfully and wonderfully made. David praised the God who had created him with such love, knowledge, and skill. Libraries of books have been written on the physiological workings of the human body. David recognized that God had designed and formed his very existence.

PSALM 139:15
the miracle of birth

secret place ... depths of the earth. David is referring to the womb. It is called the *secret place* because the development of the fetus happens in a concealed manner and was quite mysterious to those in David's day. The womb is likened to the *depths of the earth* where darkness, dampness, and separation are brought to mind. For David to have been formed in a place where life did not exist was an amazing thought to him.

PSALM 139:16

All the days ordained. The idea is that a person's life is brought about only by the sovereign plan of God. Our time on this earth is completely in His hands, decided by our all-knowing God before our birth.

[1] Dr. H.L. Wilmington, *Wilmington's Guide to the Bible* (Wheaton, IL: Tyndale House Publishers, Inc.).

Session

2

My Personality

Prepare for the Session

	READINGS	REFLECTIVE QUESTIONS
Monday	Genesis 25:21	Think of a specific prayer request you made on someone's behalf. How did God answer?
Tuesday	Genesis 25:22	When have you asked God why something was happening to you? What response did you get?
Wednesday	Genesis 25:23–27	What unique qualities and interests has God given you?
Thursday	Genesis 25:29–34	Have you ever "despised" one of God's gifts to you? Why or why not?
Friday	Genesis 33:1	Who do you need to reconcile with? Pray for that person and for wisdom on how to begin the process of reconciliation.
Saturday	Genesis 33:4	How do you respond to people who have harmed you?
Sunday	Genesis 33:10	How is reconciling with someone like "seeing the face of God"?

notes:

OUR GOALS FOR THIS SESSION ARE:

⊌ **In groups of 6–8, gather people in a horseshoe configuration.**

Make sure everyone has a name tag.

Take time to share information on class parties that are coming up as well as any relevant church events.

INTRODUCE THE ICEBREAKER ACTIVITY: The students have been given instructions in their books.

After the Icebreaker say something like, "While we may want to be invulnerable super beings, in reality we have many human weaknesses. To share with other vulnerable human beings and have an influence on them, we have to be willing to be vulnerable ourselves. In this session we will look at what this means for us."

Hand out the Prayer/Praise Report. A sample copy is on pages 158-159. Have people write down prayer requests and praises. Then have the prayer coordinator collect the report and make copies for use during the Caring Time.

BIBLE STUDY
- to understand that God has made each person with a unique personality
- to recognize that God uses different personalities in ministry
- to understand the importance of celebrating differences instead of criticizing them

LIFE CHANGE
- to accept personality differences in others
- to interact with different personalities
- to find a ministry that best fits our unique personalities

2

Icebreaker (10-15 minutes)

Follow the Leader! Have you ever noticed that some people approach vacations differently than others? Imagine that your family or friends are accompanying you on a vacation at the beach. You have been given the responsibility of being the trip leader. Which of the following would most accurately describe your behavior? Pick one in each group.

1. We'll leave sometime tomorrow between sunrise and sunset. *OR* We're leaving at 8:00 a.m. sharp with or without you!

2. We'll stop whenever any of you need to; we've got plenty of time. *OR* Go now, 'cause we're not stopping until we get there!

3. We'll find a place to stay when we get there. *OR* Last year I called the Chamber of Commerce for all their condominium brochures. I've had a reservation for 11 months.

4. I know there are plenty of sights to see, but we'll just major on relaxation. *OR* Here's the schedule for tomorrow, memorize it. We can't waste any time if we want to take it all in.

5. I think we'll go to a secluded beach where we can be alone and relax. *OR* We're going to the most popular beach where all the excitement and activity is.

Bible Study (30-45 minutes)

The Scripture for this week:

LEARNING FROM
THE BIBLE

GENESIS 25:21–34;

**Have two members
of the class, selected
ahead of time, read
the two passages
from Genesis.**

²¹*Isaac prayed to the Lord on behalf of his wife, because she was barren. The Lord answered his prayer, and his wife Rebekah became pregnant.* ²²*The babies jostled each other within her, and she said, "Why is this happening to me?" So she went to inquire of the Lord.*

²³*The Lord said to her, "Two nations are in your womb, and two peoples from within you will be separated; one people will be stronger than the other, and the older will serve the younger."*

²⁴*When the time came for her to give birth, there were twin boys in her womb.* ²⁵*The first to come out was red, and his whole body was like a hairy garment; so they named him Esau.* ²⁶*After this, his brother came out, with his hand grasping Esau's heel; so he was named Jacob. Isaac was sixty years old when Rebekah gave birth to them.*

²⁷*The boys grew up, and Esau became a skillful hunter, a man of the open country, while Jacob was a quiet man, staying among the tents.* ²⁸*Isaac, who had a taste for wild game, loved Esau, but Rebekah loved Jacob.*

²⁹*Once when Jacob was cooking some stew, Esau came in from the open country, famished.* ³⁰*He said to Jacob, "Quick, let me have some of that red stew! I'm famished!" (That is why he was also called Edom.)*

³¹*Jacob replied, "First sell me your birthright."*

³²*"Look, I am about to die," Esau said. "What good is the birthright to me?"*

³³*But Jacob said, "Swear to me first." So he swore an oath to him, selling his birthright to Jacob.*

³⁴*Then Jacob gave Esau some bread and some lentil stew. He ate and drank, and then got up and left. So Esau despised his birthright.*

GENESIS 33:1,4,10

¹*Jacob looked up and there was Esau, coming with his four hundred men; ...*

⁴*But Esau ran to meet Jacob and embraced him; he threw his arms around his neck and kissed him. And they wept. ...*

¹⁰*"No, please!" said Jacob. "If I have found favor in your eyes, accept this gift from me. For to see your face is like seeing the face of God, now that you have received me favorably."*

notes:

...about today's session (5 minutes)

YOU'VE GOT PERSONALITY

Summarize these introductory remarks. Be sure to include the underlined information, which gives the answers to the student book questions (provided in the margin).

What is a personality? Personality is seen in the way we think, feel, and act. <u>Some scientists say they've identified as many as 18,000 different personality traits</u>. Each of us has a different combination of those traits. We were born with some of these traits while others were partially learned.

How many different personality traits have scientists identified?

We are complex individuals. Our personalities affect every area of our lives: how we respond to change, how we solve problems, the type of work we enjoy, how we respond to conflict, how we relate to God, and how we get along with other people. Often, we are misunderstood because of personality differences. We need to understand our own personalities and be sensitive to the personalities of others. Proverbs 19:11 says, "A man's wisdom gives him patience; it is to his glory to overlook an offense." The more you understand a person, the more understanding you become.

Knowing your temperament will also help you find the place of ministry that best fits you. For example, an introverted person is not best suited to be a door greeter. And, a detail-oriented person is probably not the best person to serve on a "Dream Big" vision team.

Scientists and psychologists have developed many tests to determine or classify personalities. Here's a widely used classification of personalities. Determine which one best describes your personality.

Which temperament category best describes your personality?

1. <u>SANGUINE</u>—outgoing, optimistic, life of the party, outspoken, witty, easygoing

Each group member will identify one of the four underlined options.

2. <u>CHOLERIC</u>—outgoing, optimistic, outspoken, type A, tend to be bossy and demanding, decisive

3. <u>MELANCHOLY</u>—introverted, pessimistic, organized, detailed, makes lists, goal-oriented

4. <u>PHLEGMATIC</u>—introverted, pessimistic, steady, dependable, team player, not goal-oriented, resist conflict and change

This gives you an idea of how different we can be! Did you determine which one sounded most like you? There is not a right or wrong personality. Each has its strengths and weaknesses. God wants us to understand our differences and find out how to use our personalities effectively in ministry.

How can you use your personality strengths for God's work?

Today, we'll look at the story of twin brothers: Jacob and Esau. We will see how different their personalities were and how we can more effectively relate to persons whose personalities differ from our own.

notes:

✝

Identifying with the Story (5-7 minutes)

♆ **Remain in groups of 6–8 people, in a horseshoe configuration.**

In this small-group session, students will be responding to the following questions that will help them share their stories in terms of the story about Jacob and Esau in Genesis.

Have the students explore these questions together.

1. Jacob and Esau were twin brothers, but they had very different personalities. Choosing from the following list of personality traits, which ones most closely describe Jacob (mark with a "J")? Esau (mark with an "E")? You (mark with a "Y")?

___ outgoing   ___ competitive
___ reserved   ___ controlled
___ thinker   ___ expressive
___ feeler   ___ likes routine
___ cooperative   ___ likes variety

2. In reference to the personality development of Jacob and Esau, place the following factors in order of their influence on these two brothers—with 1 being the most influential and 5 being the least influential.

Jacob	Esau
___ physical appearance	___ physical appearance
___ Isaac (father)	___ Isaac (father)
___ Rebekah (mother)	___ Rebekah (mother)
___ God	___ God
___ birth order	___ birth order

3. In Genesis 33, we see Jacob and Esau reconciling their relationship. What is the biggest factor that keeps people from reconciling broken relationships?

☐ hope the situation will work itself out
☐ desire to get revenge
☐ reluctance to admit wrong
☐ fear of appearing weak
☐ fear of confrontation
☐ other:_____

notes:

Share with your class the following information which you may modify according to your own perspectives and teaching needs. The answers to the student book questions (provided in the margin) are underlined.

What are three truths that show the importance of understanding our personalities?

God created us with:

today's session (15-20 minutes)

In our two passages we see some truths that will help us realize the importance of understanding our personalities. Let's look at three of these truths.

God Created Us with Unique Personalities

In Genesis 25:23, we see that God had shaped Jacob's and Esau's personalities. While they were in their mother's womb, God gave them certain tendencies unique to each. In Romans 9:11-12, Paul reveals his awareness of God's personal involvement in the lives of Jacob and Esau. "Before the twins were born or had done anything good or bad—in order that God's purpose in election might stand: not by works but by him who calls—she was told, 'The older will serve the younger.' "

Based on Psalm 139, we know that God fashions and shapes us from the moment of conception. In Genesis 25:27, we learn of some specifics concerning the personalities of these twins: "The boys grew up, and Esau became a skillful hunter, a man of the open country, while Jacob was a quiet man, staying among the tents."

In today's society, Jacob would probably enjoy working in a cubicle doing a job that didn't require a high volume of interaction with other people. Esau would most likely find a job working outdoors. You can probably look at your own family and see how unique the personalities are even among brothers and sisters.

We need to understand that God makes each person unique—even twins. For those of you who are married, more than likely you married someone who has the opposite personality from you. One of you thrives in structure and routine while the other likes variety and adventure. One of you may freely reveal your emotions while the other conceals feelings.

today's session (cont'd)

God Uses Heredity and Environment to Shape Our Personalities

The personalities of Jacob and Esau were influenced by several factors. One of those factors was heredity. Whether we like it or not, we tend to resemble our parents. These physical traits can influence our personalities. In Genesis 25:25–28, we learn that Esau had darker skin that was covered by a large amount of hair. Almost everyone would agree that physical appearance can influence how we see ourselves. If someone is not content with his or her physical appearance, insecurities and a lack of confidence can develop.

Another factor that can shape one's personality is the personality of his or her parents. In Genesis 25:27–30, we see that their parents had a major influence on the lives of Jacob and Esau. Isaac favored Esau and it showed. Isaac loved to eat wild game and apparently spent time with Esau showing him how to hunt. Rebekah favored Jacob and it showed. Rebekah apparently spent time with her quieter son, showing him how to cook. Even though they were twins, Esau was adventurous and expressive while Jacob was an indoor type of person, a man of thought more than action.

God uses our:

God Uses Our Unique Personalities for His Purposes

Can you imagine a world where everyone had the same likes and dislikes? What if everyone responded to every problem in the same way? First, this would be a boring place! And second, nothing would get done! We need certain types of personalities to do certain kinds of jobs. Not everyone has the personality to work on an assembly line and not everyone has the personality to be a news reporter. God loves variety and creates different personalities to accomplish certain tasks in His kingdom.

How did God use Peter's personality to accomplish His purposes?

Just look at Jesus' disciples. Peter certainly had a different personality than most of the other disciples. Peter was outgoing and brash. He wanted to take over the situation, even trying to correct Jesus (Matt. 16:22): "Peter took him aside and began to rebuke him, 'Never, Lord!' he said, 'This shall never happen to you!' " <u>What was a personality flaw in Peter, God turned into a strength. God used his boldness and fierce loyalty to proclaim the good news of Jesus Christ to thousands at Pentecost</u> (Acts 2:14).

As you've probably experienced in your own relationships, conflict can easily arise between people with different personalities. This is the challenge many couples face today. During dating, they learn that opposites attract. After the wedding, opposites attack! Personality differences can also create conflicts that result in sibling rivalries. In Genesis 25:29–34, Jacob takes advantage of Esau's impulsive nature by making an impromptu deal for Esau's birthright. In Genesis 33:1–10, Esau and Jacob reconcile their broken relationship.

As believers today, we must realize that God has made each of us different. We shouldn't expect everyone to think, act, or respond as we do. Learning to accept, appreciate, and relate to different personalities is important in our efforts to work as a team in the body of Christ to accomplish His purposes.

Personality is one factor we should consider when looking for a place to serve. God wants us to understand our personality and find the place of ministry that best suits us. God made you a certain way and developed the personality you have for a reason. Do you see it as an area of tremendous potential? Are you living up to that potential?

notes:

✝

Remain in groups of 6–8 people, in a horseshoe configuration.

In this small-group session, students will be applying the lessons of the text to their own lives through the following questions.

The students were asked (in the student book) to choose an answer for each question and explain why.

Learning from the Story (5-7 minutes)

1. Esau's personality was similar to his father's. Jacob's was similar to his mother's. Of the members of your family, which one are you most like? List three ways you are similar in personality.

2. Esau made a hasty decision to trade his birthright for food. Describe a hasty decision you've made that turned out to be a poor choice. What would you do differently?

3. What is the greatest strength of your personality? Name three ministries in your church that could benefit from this strength.

notes:

life change lessons (5-7 minutes)

Accept _____ in others.

Interact with _____.

Find a ministry that _____.

Make a list of your personality traits.

Strengths:

Weaknesses:

As we have seen in our groups, God created each of us with a unique personality. Here are three keys on how to make the most of our personality differences:

1. <u>ACCEPT PERSONALITY DIFFERENCES IN OTHERS.</u> Not everyone thinks as you do. Some think in concrete terms while others think in more abstract ways. Everyone doesn't feel emotions as you do. Under stress, this really becomes evident. Some laugh while others cry. Some become boisterous while others clam up. The sooner we recognize, understand, and accept the personality differences in others, the better we'll get along. When we understand how a person is "wired," the less we'll be surprised by his or her actions and reactions. And the better we'll be able to work together.

2. <u>INTERACT WITH DIFFERENT PERSONALITIES</u>. In Romans 15:7, Paul instructs us to, "Accept one another." The best way to get along with different personalities is to accept the differences and refuse to criticize how someone else thinks, responds, acts, or reacts to a situation. Instead, we should learn to appreciate all of the different personalities God has placed within the body of Christ. We can have unity in the body of Christ without uniformity.

3. <u>FIND A MINISTRY THAT BEST FITS YOUR UNIQUE PERSONALITY</u>. Make a list of the personality traits you consider strengths and a list of personality traits you consider weaknesses. Ask yourself what your personality indicates about the type of ministry God wants you to be involved with. For example, if you're an extrovert, greeting people at the door will probably be easier for you than serving as the librarian.

notes:

Caring Time (15-20 minutes)

⟳ CARING TIME
Remain in groups
of 6–8 people, in
a horseshoe
configuration.

Hand out the Prayer/
Praise Report to the
entire group. Ask
each subgroup to
pray for the empty
chair. Pray specifically
for God to guide you
to someone to bring
next week to fill
that chair.

After a sufficient
time of prayer in
subgroups, close in a
corporate prayer. Say,
"Next week we will
talk about: 'What Are
My Special Talents?' "

Remind participants
of the daily Scripture
readings and
reflective questions
found on page 32.

Have members pray for the person on their right, using the concerns listed on the Prayer/Praise Report. Also, pray that this person would understand how to use his or her personality to serve God most effectively.

Close by thanking God for bringing you together as a group and for the different personalities that form the body of Christ.

notes:

Reference Notes

Use these notes to gain further understanding
of the text as you study on your own.

BIBLE STUDY NOTES

GENESIS 25:22
a struggle

jostled each other. The future struggle between the Edomites and the Israelites is foreshadowed here in Rebekah's womb. The nation of Edom was comprised of Esau's descendants and the nation of Israel was comprised of Jacob's descendants.

GENESIS 25:23
cultural break

the older will serve the younger. Under normal circumstances, cultural law gave the older son preeminence over a younger son. God, however, had other plans for these two brothers (see Rom. 9:10–13).

GENESIS 25:25

red. Esau's other name is Edom which means "red" (see v. 30).

GENESIS 25:26

Jacob. "Heel catcher," "supplanter" or "trickster." Figuratively, it means "he deceives," a foreshadowing of how he treated his blind father to secure the blessing of the firstborn (Gen. 27).

GENESIS 25:31
birthright

sell me your birthright. In ancient times, the birthright assured the eldest son a double portion of his father's inheritance.

GENESIS 25:33

Swear to me first. The birthright could be legally forfeited through a verbal oath.

GENESIS 25:34

Esau despised his birthright. Esau proved himself to be "godless" (see Heb. 12:16) by sacrificing God's blessings for a single meal.

GENESIS 33:4
eager reconciliation

Esau ran to meet Jacob and embraced him. This was not at all what Jacob expected from Esau, evidenced by Jacob's protective arranging of his family. Apparently, God had been at work in Esau's heart to the point where he no longer held a grudge against Jacob.

2

notes:

Session

3

What Are My Special Talents?

Prepare for the Session

	READINGS	REFLECTIVE QUESTIONS
Monday	Exodus 31:1–2	What gifts has God chosen to give you?
Tuesday	Exodus 31:3–5	Why is it important to realize that God chooses to give us certain gifts and not others?
Wednesday	Exodus 31:6–7	God chose Bezalel to lead and Oholiab to help. When has God called you to help someone else?
Thursday	1 Corinthians 10:31	Think of your daily activities. How can you use them "to the glory of God"?
Friday	Matthew 25:14–29	Examine how you have utilized your gifts. Do you think you will be given greater opportunities for service or less? Why?
Saturday	John 15:5	When have you tried to do something that wasn't in God's plan for you?
Sunday	John 1:14	Who is Jesus to you?

notes:

**OUR GOALS FOR
THIS SESSION ARE:**

In groups of 6–8,
gather people in
a horseshoe
configuration.

Make sure everyone
has a name tag.

Take time to share
information on class
parties that are coming
up as well as any
relevant church events.

**INTRODUCE THE
ICEBREAKER ACTIVITY:**
The students have
been given instructions
in their books.

After the Icebreaker
say something like,
"More than likely,
you prefer an activity
that compliments
your greatest talent
or ability. God expects
us to use our talents
and abilities for His
glory. In today's
session, we'll take
a look at how God
wants to use those
talents and abilities
to fulfill His plan."

Hand out the
Prayer/Praise Report.
A sample copy is
on pages 158-159.
Have people write
down prayer requests
and praises. Then
have the prayer
coordinator collect
the report and make
copies for use during
the Caring Time.

BIBLE STUDY
- to realize that our talents and abilities are given to us by God
- to understand that God can use our talents for His glory
- to understand how our talents enable us to fulfill God's plan
- to learn the importance of using the talents God has given us

LIFE CHANGE
- to make a realistic assessment of our talents and abilities by listing our strengths and weaknesses
- to develop our talents and abilities by making a plan to learn and grow
- to use our talents and abilities in ministry

3

Icebreaker   (10-15 minutes)

Shipwreck. Your group has been shipwrecked on a deserted island. The first thought on everyone's mind is survival. As a group you decide that each person should be given a job to do. Which one of the following would you choose and why (place a ✓ in the box)? Which one of the following would you least want to do and why (place an X in the box)?

- ☐ design and build a boat
- ☐ hunt for food
- ☐ cook the food
- ☐ plan the agenda for the day
- ☐ entertain the group so they won't be bored
- ☐ write a letter to be placed in a bottle to be thrown out to sea
- ☐ decorate the inside of the hut that will be built
- ☐ run all over the island, scout it out, and report back to the group as quickly as possible
- ☐ organize supplies and keep track of how long food and water rations will last

notes:

notes:

LEARNING FROM THE BIBLE

EXODUS 31:1–7

Have a member of the class, selected ahead of time, read the passage from Exodus.

Bible Study (30-45 minutes)

The Scripture for this week:

¹Then the Lord said to Moses, ²"See, I have chosen Bezalel son of Uri, the son of Hur, of the tribe of Judah, ³and I have filled him with the Spirit of God, with skill, ability and knowledge in all kinds of crafts—⁴to make artistic designs for work in gold, silver and bronze, ⁵to cut and set stones, to work in wood, and to engage in all kinds of craftsmanship. ⁶Moreover, I have appointed Oholiab son of Ahisamach, of the tribe of Dan, to help him. Also I have given skill to all the craftsmen to make everything I have commanded you: ⁷the Tent of Meeting, the ark of the Testimony with the atonement cover on it, and all the other furnishings of the tent."

notes:

...about today's session (5 minutes)

KNOW YOUR ABILITIES

It's obvious that God gave each of us different abilities in life. None of us are exactly alike. <u>The most obvious way we're different is physically.</u> By looking at a person's height, you can tell that some people are just meant to play basketball while others are meant to jockey horses in the Kentucky Derby. Some people have a knack for working with their hands while others thrive by using their brains to analyze, engineer, and organize. Some people are created with the ability to sing and play instruments while others are gifted artistically. Some people are better speakers while others are better writers.

God has designed each of us with the ability to excel in certain areas. We must be careful not to force individuals into a mold that doesn't fit their abilities and talents. The result will most certainly be frustration and failure.

<u>Researchers tell us that the average person has at least 500 abilities.</u> The key is to use as many of these abilities as possible <u>to glorify God</u>. You may have been born with some of these abilities and others God may have developed in you through years in an occupation. You need to think about the skills you would include on your resumé and how you could use them for God.

Today, we'll look at how God gave certain individuals specific abilities to accomplish the building project He gave Moses. We'll find that God's calling on our lives and our God-given abilities and talents often match perfectly.

notes:

Summarize these introductory remarks. Be sure to include the underlined information, which gives the answers to the student book questions (provided in the margin).

What is the most obvious way each human is different?

How many abilities does the average person have?

What has God called you to do with the abilities He's given you?

3

35

✝

Identifying with the Story (5-7 minutes)

Remain in groups of 6–8 people, in a horseshoe configuration.

In this small-group session, students will be responding to the following questions that will help them share their stories in terms of talents and abilities God gave Moses and Bezalel.

Have the students explore these questions together.

1. What was the main reason God did not choose Moses to build the tabernacle himself?

   ☐ He wouldn't have the time to do it.
   ☐ He didn't have the skill to do it.
   ☐ God wanted to show the value of teamwork.
   ☐ He didn't have enough experience in crafts.
   ☐ Moses was better at working with people than his hands.
   ☐ Other: _____

2. God gave Bezalel exceptional skill and ability in all kinds of crafts. God then used his skills to build the tabernacle. Of the following areas, where do you think your greatest talent or ability lies?

   ☐ working with my hands   ☐ writing
   ☐ working with numbers   ☐ art
   ☐ problem solving   ☐ designing
   ☐ organizing and planning   ☐ music
   ☐ working with people   ☐ public speaking
   ☐ sports/athletic ability   ☐ other:_____

3. In the same way God used Bezalel and his skills to accomplish His plan, God desires to use your talents and abilities. What is the first thought that comes to your mind about using your abilities and skills for God in ministry?

   ☐ I'm too busy.
   ☐ I don't see how my occupational skills can be used for God's glory.
   ☐ I don't have any special talents or abilities.
   ☐ No one will take me seriously.
   ☐ I need someone to help me find a way to use my talents in ministry.
   ☐ I am currently using my natural abilities in ministry as I _____.
   ☐ I've never really thought about it. I need to pray about it.

notes:

today's session (15-20 minutes)

Share with your class the following information which you may modify according to your own perspectives and teaching needs. The answers to the student book questions (provided in the margin) are underlined.

What are four truths associated with God's desire to use our talents and abilities?

Talents and abilities are:

What Old Testament story illustrates the consequences of using our abilities for selfish purposes rather than in obedience to God?

In today's passage we see some important truths that will help us understand God's desire to use the talents He's given us for His glory. Let's look at four of these truths.

Talents and Abilities Are Given to Us by God

In Exodus 31:3, we see that Bezalel's abilities as a craftsman were given to him by God. God gives each of us certain abilities at birth, but talents and abilities can be wasted on worldly pursuits. Apart from the Spirit's work in our lives, all we do is "of the flesh." Bezalel didn't just have skills and abilities. He had the Spirit of God energizing his work, and he willingly used his skills for God, not himself.

In contrast, <u>one of the saddest verses in the Bible comes out of the Old Testament story of Samson and Delilah</u>. God had blessed Samson with great physical strength, but he served his own fleshly desires that were not in line with God's directives. By doing this, he betrayed God's gift to him. Samson allowed his hair to be cut which broke a Nazarite vow he had made to God. The result was that God's presence and power were taken from him. "Then she [Delilah] called, 'Samson, the Philistines are upon you!' He awoke from his sleep and thought, 'I'll go out as before and shake myself free.' But he did not know that the Lord had left him" (Judg. 16:20). We must be careful never to take for granted our skills and abilities. And, we must also make sure we are obedient to God.

God gives each of us certain abilities at birth. Some people are given hands that can perform delicate surgeries. Some people have a natural way with words and write books. Others develop skills that don't come naturally but are gained through training, education, and experience. While many skills must be developed through persistent practice, God is the ultimate source of our talents and abilities. Whatever talents and abilities we have, we need to remember that God created us with the capacity to learn, develop, master, and use those skills. Our natural abilities are much like spiritual gifts in that both come from God and are to be used for God. As we hear and do those things the Holy Spirit prompts us to do, God will use our natural abilities and talents for His purposes.

God can use our talents and abilities for:

God Can Use Our Talents and Abilities for His Glory

God's ultimate purpose for the tabernacle was to bring honor and glory to His name. The tabernacle represented God's presence among His people. Each of the craftsmen involved in this project were being used of God for His glory. In 1 Corinthians 10:31, we learn that God wants us to apply all our abilities in ways that glorify

today's session (cont'd)

him: "Whether you eat or drink or whatever you do, do it all for the glory of God."

Many of us tend to underestimate our talents and abilities. We think that the skills we use at work can only be used in that type of industry. We limit our usefulness to God by our small thinking. The Book of Psalms has been called the hymn book of Israel. It contains many songs and prayers written by David who was talented with playing the harp. Because David didn't limit God by small thinking and he allowed God to use his musical abilities, we have this great source of inspiration, wisdom, and comfort.

How do we limit God's use of our talents and abilities?

Our Talents and Abilities Complement God's Plan for Our Lives

Our talents and abilities complement:

God will never ask us to do anything He doesn't equip and empower us to do. The abilities we have aren't an accident of fate. For example, King David learned how to defeat a giant named Goliath as a shepherd boy who protected his flock from wild animals. The apostle Paul debated and explained that Jesus was the Messiah to Jews and Gentiles from his vast knowledge of the Old Testament and oratory skills developed while he was an unbeliever. For 40 years, Moses learned the skills of shepherding animals in a region that would one day be the place where he would lead his people out of Egyptian bondage. A good indicator of God's will for our lives is the abilities and skills He's given us. God placed us here on earth for a purpose. Our abilities show us a great deal about how He wants us to serve Him.

What is a good indicator of God's will for our lives?

God Expects Us to Use the Talents and Abilities He Has Given Us

God expects us to:

If we don't use the talents and abilities God has given us, we will lose them. In Matthew 25:28, Jesus said this concerning the wicked and lazy servant: " 'Take the talent from him and give it to the parable is a particular sum of money, the principle remains the same: God expects a return on His investment, whether it's money or the abilities that He's given us. God has the right to take them back if we waste them.

What will happen if we don't use the talents and abilities God has given us?

Know that God holds us accountable for what we do with the abilities and skills we are given. While we may not be given the task of building a tabernacle, we have been given the task of building the body of Christ. We have talents that God can use if we step out and give them to God. Some of you may be thinking that you're already using your talents and skills in your area of employment. That may be true, but we need to make sure that we are open to God's leadership for how we can be faithful in creatively using those abilities for Him.

notes:

Remain in groups of 6–8 people, in a horseshoe configuration.

In this small-group session, students will be applying the lessons of the text to their own lives through the following questions.

The students were asked (in the student book) to choose an answer for each question and explain why.

3

Learning from the Story (5-7 minutes)

1. In this passage, we see how God gave people special talents and abilities and then matched the people with the work He wanted them to do. Have you ever had a job or volunteered to do something but later quit because it didn't fit you? What is an activity you've done within the last week that displays a skill or ability you have?

2. What does the phrase found in Exodus 31:3, "I have filled him with the Spirit of God" and John 15:5, "apart from me you can do nothing" tell us about the manner in which God will use our talents and abilities?

3. List your top three talents, natural abilities, or job skills. Name three ministries in your church that could benefit from them.

notes:

life change lessons (5-7 minutes)

Share with the class the following thoughts on how the lessons of this text might be applied today. The answers to the student book questions (provided in the margin) are underlined unless the question requires a personal answer.

What are three steps for using your talents and abilities for the purpose of ministry?

1. _____ of your talents and abilities.

2. _____ your talents and abilities.

3. Use your talents and abilities _____.

What is your plan for developing and improving your abilities and talents?

As we have seen in our groups, God has given each of us talents and abilities to be used in ministry. Here are three steps for using our talents and abilities for the purpose of ministry:

1. <u>MAKE A REALISTIC ASSESSMENT OF YOUR TALENTS AND ABILITIES BY LISTING YOUR STRENGTHS AND WEAKNESSES.</u> Unfortunately, many of us don't know what we're good at because we do those things without much effort. We tend to recognize those things that we don't do well because that's what we stress out about. Ask a friend, family member, or coworker to list your top five talents or abilities. You make a list as well, then compare the two. See if there are any similarities or differences. The point of this is to target some God-given abilities that you can use for God.

2. <u>DEVELOP YOUR TALENTS AND ABILITIES</u> BY MAKING A PLAN TO LEARN AND GROW. In Ecclesiastes 10:10, we learn a valuable truth: "If the ax is dull and its edge unsharpened, more strength is needed but skill will bring success." You need to work on sharpening and improving the skills you have. In doing so, you will be more effective in service. You may need to take some courses, read some books, practice more often, listen to tapes, talk to experts in that area, etc. Never stop learning and growing. You need to take what God has given you and make the most of it. What is your plan for developing your abilities and talents?

3. <u>USE YOUR TALENTS AND ABILITIES IN MINISTRY.</u> You may be thinking, "The abilities and skills I use at work have no place in church service." That's not true. Those talents and abilities and skills are needed. God placed you in your church because your abilities can help achieve His plan there. Don't deny the body of Christ the benefit of your skills. Let them know of your abilities and willingness to serve. Even if you don't see a place of ministry that fits your primary talents and abilities, you need to serve anyway. You can't sit back and wait for the perfect opportunity because you may never find it. God expects you to start serving now, wherever the need is. As you do, it will become obvious over time how your skills can be used to the fullest.

notes:

Caring Time   (15-20 minutes)

Take time to pray for one another and for your own special concerns. Pray that all of the group members will use their talents for God's glory. Also, pray for the concerns and requests listed on the Prayer/Praise Report.

Close by taking a few minutes for each group member to offer a brief prayer of thanksgiving for the abilities and talents that God has graciously and lovingly given to him or her.

notes:

BIBLE STUDY NOTES

Reference Notes

Use these notes to gain further understanding
of the text as you study on your own.

EXODUS 31:2
a craftsman

Bezalel. His name means "in the shadow of God" or "under the protection of God."

EXODUS 31:3
God-given

I have filled him with the Spirit of God. Bezalel's talents can be attributed directly to the enabling work of God. God gave him the skills, ability, and knowledge to do this kind of work and the desire to use his gifts for God's glory.

EXODUS 31:6
helper

Oholiab. His name means, "The Father is my tabernacle." God chose Oholiab to be Bezalel's helper in building the tabernacle.

EXODUS 31:7
tabernacle

Tent of Meeting. Also called the tabernacle, symbolized God's presence with His people and was a picture of Christ (John 1:14), the Word who became flesh and "tabernacled" among us.

Session
4

What Does the Bible Say About Spiritual Gifts? (part 1)

Prepare for the Session

	READINGS	REFLECTIVE QUESTIONS
Monday	1 Corinthians 12:4–7	How are you using your gifts for the "common good"?
Tuesday	1 Corinthians 12:11	What does it mean to you that God picked your gifts just for you?
Wednesday	1 Peter 4:10	What does God expect you to do with the gifts He has given you?
Thursday	Matthew 20:26–28	How do you determine greatness?
Friday	Romans 12:4–8	Your gifts reveal God's grace. How do others see you using that grace on their behalf?
Saturday	Philippians 4:12–13	How contented are you with your life and the gifts God has given you?
Sunday	Matthew 25:14–29	What fears are keeping you from fully using your talents? Will God say to you, "Well done"?

notes:

OUR GOALS FOR THIS SESSION ARE:

In groups of 6–8, gather people in a horseshoe configuration.

Make sure everyone has a name tag.

Take time to share information on class parties that are coming up as well as any relevant church events.

INTRODUCE THE ICEBREAKER ACTIVITY: The students have been given instructions in their books.

After the Icebreaker say something like, "You probably talked about what items to take and why. With the right tools, the construction of the building would be much quicker and the quality of construction much better. In today's session, we're going to discuss how the Holy Spirit gives us tools (spiritual gifts) to help build up His church (the body of Christ)."

Hand out the Prayer/Praise Report. A sample copy is on pages 158-159. Have people write down prayer requests and praises. Then have the prayer coordinator collect the report and make copies for use during the Caring Time.

BIBLE STUDY
- to understand that all spiritual gifts come from God
- to realize that spiritual gifts are not for personal benefit, but for the benefit of others
- to recognize that the Holy Spirit determines the gifts we are given

LIFE CHANGE
- to appreciate believers who have different gifts than we do
- to be content with the gifts we have been given by God
- to use our spiritual gifts to minister to others on a regular basis

Icebreaker (10-15 minutes)

4

What Would You Take? Your group has traveled abroad on a mission trip to an impoverished land. The first task given to your group is to build a church building for the small group of believers there. The problem is that the people have no tools available for construction and only limited construction materials such as trees, clay, water, nails, etc. Your group can only take three of the following items into the village where the building is to be built. Decide as a group which three items you would take to use as tools for constructing the building.

- ☐ a glass, gallon milk jug
- ☐ a pitchfork
- ☐ a dull butter knife
- ☐ a five-iron golf club
- ☐ a queen-size cotton bed sheet
- ☐ a 50-yard ball of yarn
- ☐ a roll of aluminum foil
- ☐ a dull ax
- ☐ duct tape

notes:

notes:

**LEARNING FROM
THE BIBLE**

**1 CORINTHIANS
12:4–7,11**

**Have one class
member, selected
ahead of time,
read the passage
from 1 Corinthians.**

Bible Study   (30-45 minutes)

The Scripture for this week:

⁴*There are different kinds of gifts, but the same Spirit.* ⁵*There are different kinds of service, but the same Lord.* ⁶*There are different kinds of working, but the same God works all of them in all men.*

⁷*Now to each one the manifestation of the Spirit is given for the common good. ...* ¹¹*All these are the work of one and the same Spirit, and he gives them to each one, just as he determines.*

notes:

...about today's session (5 minutes)

BETTER THAN CHRISTMAS

Spiritual gifts are often treated like toys given to children at Christmas. New gifts coming into the church are the focus of attention and actually get some use ... for maybe a week. <u>What was once a source of joy and excitement is forgotten</u>. This leaves many Christians with spiritual gifts that are untapped and underutilized. Today, we will learn what God's Word, the Bible, has to say about the use of spiritual gifts. Does God want us to allow our giftedness to be forgotten like a new toy that soon loses its excitement? What does God have to say in His Word about spiritual gifts?

Unfortunately, some of you may feel a twinge of hesitation about plunging into the topic because you've seen or heard about the misuses of spiritual gifts. <u>Spiritual gifts can be a scary topic to some Christians because they don't understand what the Bible has to say about them</u>. Instead of searching Scripture to understand spiritual gifts, some Christians find it easier to just avoid the subject. It is true that there has been some abuse and misinterpretation of the Bible concerning spiritual gifts—even by well-intentioned believers. But, that shouldn't stop us from understanding God's plan for using spiritual gifts in our lives. In our next two sessions, we'll look at what God's Word has to say about spiritual gifts and how He wants us to use them.

Today, we'll see that God is in the building business. He acts as the construction superintendent who supplies His workers (individual believers) with tools (spiritual gifts) <u>so we can minister to the needs of others</u>. According to 1 Peter 4:10, "Each one should use whatever gift he has received to serve others." Because each follower of Christ has been gifted by the Holy Spirit to do a task well, every Christian is a "10" at something. Through the Holy Spirit, we are given the supernatural ability to impact the lives of those around us. In today's passage, we'll look at God's purpose for using spiritual gifts in the lives of believers and their ministry to others.

notes:

Margin notes:

Summarize these introductory remarks. Be sure to include the underlined information, which gives the answers to the student book questions (provided in the margin).

How are spiritual gifts often like toys given to children at Christmas?

Why is the topic of spiritual gifts a scary topic to some Christians?

4

Why does God give each believer spiritual gifts?

Remain in groups of 6–8 people, in a horseshoe configuration.

In this small-group session, students will be responding to the following questions that will help them share their stories in terms of the apostle Paul's words in 1 Corinthians 12:4–7,11.

Have the students explore these questions together.

Identifying with the Story (5-7 minutes)

1. Share some examples of how your love for the individuals listed below could be displayed in different ways.

   ☐ spouse_____
   ☐ close friend_____
   ☐ brother or sister_____
   ☐ child_____
   ☐ parent_____
   ☐ in-law_____
   ☐ cousin_____
   ☐ pet _____

2. Suppose you were shopping for a birthday gift for someone in your family. Which type of gift would you consider buying and why?

   ☐ something they can use but isn't very exciting
   ☐ something they really want but don't really need
   ☐ something that costs more than it's really worth
   ☐ something I want but I'm not sure if they want it
   ☐ something that's on sale
   ☐ something unusual
   ☐ something that shows I put a lot of thought into it

3. The apostle Paul writes in today's passage that God gives a variety of gifts. In which of the following areas would you rather have the most variety?

   ☐ food   ☐ job responsibilities
   ☐ wardrobe   ☐ music
   ☐ television channels   ☐ friends

notes:

today's session (15-20 minutes)

Share with your class the following information which you may modify according to your own perspectives and teaching needs. The answers to the student book questions (provided in the margin) are underlined.

What are three basic truths concerning spiritual gifts that the leader talked about?

How does God give each Christian a spiritual gift or ability?

Let's begin our study by letting Paul show us in his first letter to the Corinthians some basic truths that will build a foundation for our understanding of spiritual gifts. Without a proper understanding of their giftedness as believers, Paul knew that the Corinthians would most likely misuse and confuse spiritual gifts. Let's look at three basic truths Paul clarifies for his readers and make sure each of us has a firm grasp on these in our own lives.

God Is the Source of Our Spiritual Gifts

Along with the abiding presence of the Holy Spirit, each Christian experiences the presence of the Holy Spirit in the form of spiritual gifts. In other words, God gives each Christian a supernatural ability or skill through the work of the Holy Spirit. In verse 7, Paul writes, "Now to each one the manifestation of the Spirit is given." We can't earn "greater" gifts. Paul says that the Spirit, "gives them to each one, just as he determines" (v. 11). We may be able to develop certain skills from training and experience, but spiritual gifts can only be received as a result of God's choice. This means that pastors, spouses, and parents can't determine our giftedness. And remember, when God gives us a gift, He expects a return on His investment.

What does it mean that God is the source of our spiritual gifts? If a telemarketing representative called you at home and wanted to offer you a special gift, what would be your first reaction? You would probably be skeptical. Why? Just look at the source! Life has taught us that surely there's a catch to it such as spending three hours listening to a salesperson trying to sell you a time share or a vacation package. But if a close friend or relative wanted to come over because he or she had a special gift for you, what would your reaction be? More than likely it would be totally different from the reaction you would have to a telemarketing salesperson. Because God is the source of our spiritual gifts, our reaction should be one of excitement and gratitude. We should be excited because the God of the universe has chosen to give us certain strengths to use for His purposes. And, we should be full of gratitude because He freely chose to give you and me gifts that we don't deserve!

God Gives Us Gifts for the Purpose of Serving Others

In 1 Peter 4:10, we read what God wants His children to do with the gifts He has given them: "Each one should use whatever gift he has received to serve others." Paul shows us the same truth in 1 Corinthians 12:7 by declaring that our gifts are "given for the common good." Since it is likely that the Corinthians were seeking status by

4

today's session (cont'd)

exercising "showy" gifts, Paul wanted his readers to be absolutely clear that gifts were not for the purpose of boasting or status. Rather they were to be used for serving others. Spiritual gifts are to be used <u>outwardly</u> toward others, not <u>inwardly</u> toward self. Even among His 12 disciples Jesus would have nothing to do with self-centeredness. In Matthew 20:26–28, Jesus teaches us that greatness is determined by our willingness to serve others: "Whoever wants to become great among you must be your servant, and whoever wants to be first must be your slave—just as the Son of Man did not come to be served, but to serve, and to give his life as a ransom for many."

God Works in Different Ways in Different People

In our passage today, Paul also addressed another misunderstanding the Corinthians had about the variety of gifts. First, Paul stresses that there are a variety of gifts. "There are different kinds of gifts. ... There are different kinds of service. ... There are different kinds of working" (vv. 6–8). Second, he states that there is one God, who is the originator and orchestrator of these gifts. "But the same God works all of them in all men" (v. 6). Paul shows that our God is a God who loves variety and uses His gifts in different ways in individual lives. Notice that 1 Corinthians 12:5–8 illustrates the triune nature of God: "The same Lord ... the same God ... the same Spirit." Paul makes the point that even God works in different ways, but with one purpose. Implied in this explanation is that believers must learn the importance of serving alongside each other without jealousy or divisions.

Although there is variety in our giftedness, <u>God wants us to have unity in the body</u>. In Romans 12:5–8, Paul shows us that when each of us serves willingly and selflessly with the gifts that God has given, unity in the body is a supernatural result.

Spiritual gifts are to be used _____ toward others, not _____ toward self.

What does God want us to have in addition to a variety of gifts?

notes:

48

Remain in groups of 6–8 people, in a horseshoe configuration.

In this small-group session, students will be applying the lessons of the text to their own lives through the following questions.

The students were asked (in the student book) to choose an answer for each question and explain why.

Learning from the Story (5-7 minutes)

1. Based on the words Paul used in this passage, what was the main problem he was trying to correct among the Corinthian assembly?

   ☐ view of God—They thought there were several gods because of the variety of gifts.

   ☐ jealousy—They were jealous of others who had "showy" gifts.

   ☐ covetous—They wanted to have gifts they saw in others.

   ☐ divisions—They were excluding those who had different gifts than they did.

   ☐ status—They were elevating the importance of some gifts over others.

2. Place the following motives for using your spiritual gifts in order from "1" (best) to "5" (worst), and explain why you chose this order.

   ___ to glorify God
   ___ to help others
   ___ to live a fulfilling life
   ___ to let others see my importance
   ___ to be a good steward

3. What word below would best describe your own attitude toward others who have different spiritual gifts than you do?

   ☐ impatient   ☐ wary   ☐ cautious
   ☐ jealous   ☐ condescending   ☐ anxious
   ☐ angry   ☐ inclusive   ☐ cooperative
   ☐ immature   ☐ appreciative   ☐ other:_____

4

notes:

life change lessons (5-7 minutes)

Understanding what the Bible says about spiritual gifts can be a rewarding experience if we seek to apply the truths we learn to our lives. Let's make sure that our attitudes and motives are right by doing the following:

1. <u>APPRECIATE BELIEVERS WHO HAVE DIFFERENT GIFTS THAN YOU DO</u>. You must resist the tendency to spend most of your time with those who are gifted as you are. Instead of isolating yourself from those you may feel uncomfortable around because of their gifts, actively seek fellowship with them and allow them to encourage you in your walk with Christ. Remember, you need their giftedness and they need yours. Here's a practical way to show your appreciation: When you notice someone in your church who is faithfully using his or her gift(s), let the person know verbally or by writing a thank-you note.

2. <u>BE CONTENT WITH THE GIFTS YOU HAVE BEEN GIVEN BY GOD</u>. In a success-driven world, it is easy to slip into an unhealthy mindset toward the gifts you have. You may begin to think that if you just pray more, do more or be less sinful, God will give you what you think are "better" gifts. You need to realize that it is God's choice which gifts you receive. You should not feel unimportant or inconsequential to God's work because of the gifts you have or don't have. Your responsibility is to be a faithful steward of the gifts He has given you and to use them. If you are faithfully using your gifts in the service of others, your joy and fulfillment will be more than enough. <u>You can become dissatisfied when you stop serving others and start seeking status</u>.

3. <u>USE YOUR SPIRITUAL GIFTS TO MINISTER TO OTHERS ON A REGULAR BASIS</u>. When you are busy serving others and focusing on their needs, it becomes easier to stop complaining and coveting what others have. The solution that Paul gave the Corinthian church for their divisions and confusions included the declaration to just start serving and using the gifts that God had already given them. In what ways are you serving others on a regular basis?

notes:

Share with the class the following thoughts on how the lessons of this text might be applied today. The answers to the student book questions (provided in the margin) are underlined unless the question requires a personal answer.

What are three ways to make sure your attitude and motives are right concerning spiritual gifts?

What can cause you to become dissatisfied with the gifts you have been given by God?

♡ **CARING TIME**
Remain in groups
of 6–8 people, in
a horseshoe
configuration.

Hand out the Prayer/
Praise Report to the
entire group. Ask
each subgroup to
pray for the empty
chair. Pray specifically
for God to guide you
to someone to bring
next week to fill
that chair.

After a sufficient
time of prayer in
subgroups, close
in a corporate prayer.
Say, "Next week we
will talk about:
'What Does the Bible
Say About Spiritual
Gifts? (Part 2).' "

BIBLE STUDY NOTES

1 CORINTHIANS 12:4–6
Trinity

1 CORINTHIANS 12:4

1 CORINTHIANS 12:5
serving

1 CORINTHIANS 12:6
working

1 CORINTHIANS 12:11
chosen

Caring Time   (15-20 minutes)

Close by taking time to pray for one another and for your own special concerns. Then, pray that God would show all group members how He wants to use them to serve others. Pray that God would bring people their way who would benefit from their giftedness. Also, use the Prayer/Praise Report and pray for the concerns listed.

Conclude your prayer time by reading Psalm 100 together.

> *Shout for joy to the Lord, all the earth.*
> *Worship the Lord with gladness;*
> *come before him with joyful songs.*
> *Know that the Lord is God.*
> *It is he who made us, and we are his;*
> *we are his people, the sheep of his pasture.*
> *Enter his gates with thanksgiving*
> *and his courts with praise;*
> *give thanks to him and praise his name.*
> *For the Lord is good and his love endures forever;*
> *his faithfulness continues through all generations.*

Reference Notes

Use these notes to gain further understanding
of the text as you study on your own.

same God ... same Lord ... same Spirit. Paul mentions the three "Persons" of the Trinity to show how God works in different ways.

gifts. Certain abilities that have their source in the indwelling Holy Spirit.

service. The same word used in the first-century church for the office of deacon. This word indicates serving and meeting the needs of other Christians within the body of Christ (see Acts 6:2–3).

working. Refers to a power that is in operation and is producing results. This, no doubt, refers to the power of God working through believers to accomplish His will.

all of them in all. This expression means "all the gifts in all the persons who possess them." The phrase, "works all of them in all men," does not mean that everyone has the same gifts. In Romans 12:4, Paul clarifies that: "Each of us has one body with many members, and these members do not all have the same function."

as he determines. What gifts we have is determined by the Holy Spirit's sovereign choice. Spiritual gifts can't be selected by individuals or earned. In verses 7–11, the Spirit is referred to six times, emphasizing His sovereign control.

Session

5

What Does the Bible Say About Spiritual Gifts? (part 2)

Prepare for the Session

	READINGS	REFLECTIVE QUESTIONS
Monday	Ephesians 4:11–14	On a scale of 1 (infancy) to 10 (adulthood), what rating would you give yourself on spiritual maturity?
Tuesday	Hebrews 10:24–25	How can you encourage someone today?
Wednesday	1 Timothy 4:14	When have you neglected your spiritual gifts?
Thursday	1 Peter 4:8–11	How have you been using your gifts to serve others this week?
Friday	1 Corinthians 12:4–11	In how many ways could others benefit from your gifts?
Saturday	1 Corinthians 13:1–3	Is love for God and others your sole motivation for using your gifts? Why or why not?
Sunday	Acts 9:1–16	How does being a Christian change the way you use your gifts and talents?

notes:

**OUR GOALS FOR
THIS SESSION ARE:**

⊔ **In groups of 6–8,
gather people in
a horseshoe
configuration.**

**Make sure everyone
has a name tag.**

**Take time to share
information on class
parties that are coming
up as well as any
relevant church events.**

**INTRODUCE THE
ICEBREAKER ACTIVITY:
The students have
been given instructions
in their books.**

**After the Icebreaker
say something like,
"In today's session,
we'll look at how you
can help others grow
in spiritual maturity.
Specifically, we'll
learn how to build
up others by using
our spiritual gifts
faithfully."**

**Hand out the
Prayer/Praise Report.
A sample copy is
on pages 158-159.
Have people write
down prayer requests
and praises. Then
have the prayer
coordinator collect
the report and make
copies for use during
the Caring Time.**

BIBLE STUDY

- to understand that there is diversity in gifts but unity in purpose
- to realize that we need each other's spiritual gifts
- to recognize that using our spiritual gifts helps other Christians mature

LIFE CHANGE

- to see and appreciate how others use their gifts
- to begin serving even if we are unsure of our gifts
- to use our spiritual gifts with an attitude and motive of love

Icebreaker (10-15 minutes)

You're in the Movies. Congratulations, a screenplay about your life has been chosen by a Hollywood movie studio to be made into a motion picture! Which of the following movie titles would best describe your movie?

☐ *Scream*   ☐ *Rocky*
☐ *Beauty and the Beast*   ☐ *It's a Wonderful Life*
☐ *The Call of the Wild*   ☐ *Parent Trap*
☐ *Home Alone*   ☐ *War of the Roses*
☐ *Speed*   ☐ Other:_____

5

notes:

Bible Study (30-45 minutes)

The Scripture for this week:

¹¹It was he who gave some to be apostles, some to be prophets, some to be evangelists, and some to be pastors and teachers, ¹²to prepare God's people for works of service, so that the body of Christ may be built up ¹³until we all reach unity in the faith and in the knowledge of the Son of God and become mature, attaining to the whole measure of the fullness of Christ.

¹⁴Then we will no longer be infants, tossed back and forth by the waves, and blown here and there by every wind of teaching and by the cunning and craftiness of men in their deceitful scheming.

LEARNING FROM THE BIBLE

EPHESIANS 4:11–14

Have one class member, selected ahead of time, read the passage from Ephesians.

notes:

...about today's session (5 minutes)

OUR MUTUAL NEED

If you were to browse the "self-help" section of any bookstore, you would see hundreds of titles from, "How to Win in the Stock Market" to "How to Renovate Your Kitchen." This section is designed to help the independent person succeed in all areas of life without asking for help from a "live" person or depending on others for help. Too many Christians approach their journey in spiritual maturity like the self-help section of a bookstore. If they can just listen to the right tapes and read the right books and go to the right seminars, they can grow in their faith without the need for meaningful relationships with other believers. We can begin to think that our walk with Christ is something we can manage on our own. Scripture tells us otherwise. The writer of <u>Ecclesiastes paints a vivid picture of our need for one another (4:9–10)</u>: "Two are better than one, because they have a good return for their work: If one falls down, his friend can help him up. But pity the man who falls and has no one to help him up!"

Summarize these introductory remarks. Be sure to include the underlined information, which gives the answers to the student book questions (provided in the margin).

What self-help book(s) have you read in the last six months?

What Old Testament Scripture passage talks about our need for one another?

God intentionally designed us as Christians to need others within the context of a community of fellow believers. <u>As part of God's family we are to interact, support, and encourage each other regularly</u> (see Heb. 10:24–25).

In our passage today, we'll learn about our responsibility to build up other believers through the use of our spiritual gifts. God expects us to minister to each other's needs, both practically and spiritually, and He equips us to do so. Today, we'll look at how we contribute to the spiritual growth of other Christians as we use our spiritual gifts.

notes:

As part of God's family, what three things are we to do for other believers on a regular basis?

⊌ Remain in groups of 6–8 people, in a horseshoe configuration.

In this small-group session, students will be responding to the following questions that will help them share their stories in terms of the apostle Paul's words in Ephesians 4:11–14.

Have the students explore these questions together.

Identifying with the Story (5-7 minutes)

1. Which of the following areas of immaturity did you have the easiest time overcoming as a child? Mark it with a ✓. Which was the most difficult? Mark it with an X.

   ☐ from crawling to walking
   ☐ from being fed to feeding myself
   ☐ from crying to talking
   ☐ from wearing a diaper to being potty trained
   ☐ from being dressed to dressing myself
   ☐ from playing selfishly to playing nicely

2. If you were on a boat in the middle of the open seas during a thunderstorm, you would most likely be the person seen:

   ☐ taking a nap
   ☐ passing out life jackets
   ☐ jumping overboard to save myself
   ☐ listening closely to the instructions of the captain
   ☐ getting seasick
   ☐ letting the rain hit my face and enjoying the experience

3. In today's passage, we came across several individuals who were identified by their spiritual gifts: apostle (pioneer and church planter), prophet (motivator and encourager), evangelist (soul winner), and pastor/teacher (trainer and coach). Name a person possessing one of these gifts who has helped you grow in spiritual maturity.

5

today's session (15-20 minutes)

How is the body of Christ similar to professional sports teams?

In 1 Corinthians 7:7 and 1 Corinthians 12:29–30, what does the apostle Paul say about how Christ has distributed spiritual gifts within the body of Christ?

Professional sports teams have several things in common with the body of Christ. They have team members who play their individual positions well in addition to working together well as a team. The challenge that faces the management and coaches is pulling together a wide variety of skilled players and keeping a singular focus in front of them—winning a championship! As our manager, Christ brings together people with a variety of spiritual gifts with a singular focus—to accomplish His kingdom purposes.

Christ Distributes Spiritual Gifts for the Good of His Kingdom

From today's passage we learn that Christ has distributed spiritual gifts within the body of Christ in a way that requires every believer's participation. There's not a "Super Christian" that we can all go to for help in the areas of spiritual maturity and ministry. No one receives all the gifts. In 1 Corinthians 7:7, Paul writes, "Each man has his own gift from God; one has this gift, another has that." This means we need each others' gifts to be all God wants us to be. In our passage today, we see that Christ spreads the gifts strategically throughout the body. Paul explained that, "It was he [Christ] who gave *some* to be apostles, *some* to be prophets, *some* to be evangelists, and *some* to be pastors and teachers" (v. 11, italics added). It is also evident from this passage that no single gift is given to every believer. Nor does the Holy Spirit manifest His gifts in the same way with every believer. In 1 Corinthians 12:29–30, we read, "Are all apostles? Are all prophets? Are all teachers? Do all work miracles? Do all have gifts of healing? Do all speak in tongues? Do all interpret?" Paul's point was that no one particular gift should be expected of every believer.

Christ Desires Each of Us to Grow More Like Him Every Day

Although there is a variety and diversity of giftedness in the body of Christ, the purpose of growing more like Christ in character and conduct is to remain a unifying focus of the church. Christ desires each of us to work together as a team, using the gifts He's given us, focusing on the goal of glorifying Him by growing more like Him every day.

In Ephesians 4:11, Paul highlights some gifts that are used to build spiritual maturity in the lives of believers. The use of spiritual gifts not only equips believers to serve, it also helps develop the character and maturity needed to serve consistently and effectively. When we sit back and waste our gifts, we have more time to complain and be a source of conflict. Conversely, the natural result of everyone doing his or her part in ministry is unity and maturity. Paul urges

Using Ephesians 4:11–14, write a definition of "spiritual maturity."

each of us to keep on serving, "until we all reach *unity in the faith* and in the knowledge of the Son of God and become *mature*" (v. 13, italics added). You may ask, "What is maturity?" Paul shows us that maturity is "attaining to the whole measure of the fullness of Christ" (v. 13). Spiritual maturity is the process of becoming Christlike.

God Expects Each of Us to Do Our Part

When we keep our spiritual gifts under wraps, letting others do the work, what is the result for the church?

We need to realize that it's a sin to waste the gifts God has given us. Not only is it poor management of the spiritual gifts God has given us, it spells danger for any church. God expects us to serve with our spiritual gifts as part of the body of Christ working as it was designed (Eph. 4:16—"as each part does its work"). You get cheated when I don't use my gifts on a consistent basis, and I get cheated when you don't use your gifts on a consistent basis. We need each other's ministry.

We must remember God expects a return on the investment of spiritual gifts He's made in our lives. God has a plan for you and me to use our gifts, and He will hold us accountable. We can't pass off our gifts to another person or give them back to God. God's gifts can't be traded or exchanged. In Romans 11:29, Paul states, "God's gifts and his call are irrevocable." They are permanent. As we seek to be wise stewards of the gifts God has given us, let us strive to develop our gifts by jumping in to use them wherever there's a need and learn from others who are gifted as we are. Let's listen to Paul's instruction to his young disciple in the ministry, Timothy: "Do not neglect your gift. ... Fan into flame the gift of God, which is in you" (1 Tim. 4:14; 2 Tim. 1:6).

How can we be wise stewards of the gifts God has given us?

5

notes:

✝

U Remain in groups of 6–8 people, in a horseshoe configuration.

In this small-group session, students will be applying the lessons of the text to their own lives through the following questions.

The students were asked (in the student book) to choose an answer for each question and explain why.

Learning from the Story (5-7 minutes)

1. In this passage, Paul explains that God's people should be prepared "for works of service." What is the major reason that many Christians are not prepared to serve?

    ☐ They've never been challenged.
    ☐ They've never been encouraged.
    ☐ They've never been trained.
    ☐ They've never seen a need.
    ☐ They've always thought someone else would do it.
    ☐ They don't think they have the time.
    ☐ They don't think anyone could benefit from their ministry.
    ☐ Other: _____

2. If someone at your church approached you with an urgent need in an area you didn't feel equipped to minister in, how would you most likely respond?

    ☐ "I'll pray about it and let you know."
    ☐ "I think I know someone else who can help you."
    ☐ "I've just got too much going on right now."
    ☐ "That's not really my area of giftedness."
    ☐ "Why me?"
    ☐ "I'm still trying to figure out what my spiritual gift is. Ask me later."
    ☐ "Tell me how I can be of most help to you."
    ☐ Other: _____

3. Paul describes spiritual infants as being "tossed back and forth" and "blown here and there." What area of your spiritual life would you consider still in the infant stage?

notes:

life change lessons (5-7 minutes)

Now that we've seen what the Bible teaches about spiritual gifts, here are some steps to help you get started in using the gifts that God has given you.

Share with the class the following thoughts on how the lessons of this text might be applied today. The answers to the student book questions (provided in the margin) are underlined unless the question requires a personal answer.

What are three steps you can take to get started using the gifts God has given you?

1. SEE AND APPRECIATE HOW OTHERS USE THEIR GIFTS. Four major passages refer to spiritual gifts: Romans 12:6–8; Ephesians 4:11–16; 1 Corinthians 12–14; 1 Peter 4:10–11. One of the best ways to understand and appreciate your gifts and the gifts of others is to study these passages on spiritual gifts. You can also benefit from studying Bible characters and determining their gifts. Begin now by learning what God's Word tells us about the different ways He gifts us for service. Also, notice how others in the church serve God through their gifts.

2. BEGIN SERVING NOW EVEN IF YOU ARE UNSURE OF YOUR GIFTS. There's a phrase that's widely used in the business world that applies to the church: "Analysis Paralysis." Unfortunately, many believers hesitate to step forward and serve in ministry because they haven't discovered their gifts yet. It is unlikely that God ever intended for us to use spiritual gifts as an excuse for NOT serving. Yet, many Christians have used this excuse. If your next-door neighbor came running out of his house screaming that the house was on fire and a child was in the house, do you think the neighbor would want your help with the need at hand or wait until you knew if you were gifted enough to help? You would jump right in and help the best way you could! The world is in that kind of crisis. God wants you to start serving where the need is right now. As you begin serving, your spiritual gifts will become more evident. Many believers don't know their gifts because they have never worked with any of the ministries of their church.

What are some of the wrong motives for using your gifts to serve God and others?

3. USE YOUR SPIRITUAL GIFTS WITH AN ATTITUDE AND MOTIVE OF LOVE. You must have the right motive as you use your gifts (see 1 Cor. 13:1–3). Have you ever served because you had to? Have you ever served unwillingly? Have you ever served because someone expected you to? Have you ever served to get the applause of others? Have you ever served to gain power and control? If so, the Bible says that you've gained nothing. Let's not waste our gifts by serving with wrong motives. Let's serve out of a love for God and a love for people.

5

◡ CARING TIME
Remain in groups of 6–8 people, in a horseshoe configuration.

Hand out the Prayer/Praise Report to the entire group. Ask each subgroup to pray for the empty chair. Pray specifically for God to guide you to someone to bring next week to fill that chair.

After a sufficient time of prayer in subgroups, close in a corporate prayer. Say, "Next week we will talk about: 'What Are My Spiritual Gifts?' "

Remind participants of the daily Scripture readings and reflective questions found on page 62.

BIBLE STUDY NOTES

EPHESIANS 4:11
a gift

EPHESIANS 4:12
serve

Caring Time (15-20 minutes)

Remember that this is a time for sharing personal prayer concerns and praying for one another. Make sure to spend time praying that God will show each group member areas of need where his or her gifts can be used. Pray to always serve out of a motive of love for God and others. Also, use the Prayer/Praise Report and pray for the concerns listed.

notes:

Reference Notes

Use these notes to gain further understanding
of the text as you study on your own.

It was he who gave. The "he" here refers to Christ who, after He had ascended to the Father, gave the Person and gifts of the Holy Spirit to His followers.

to prepare God's people for works of service. The work of the church is not meant to be done by a select few. Everyone ("God's people") is to be trained to do the work.

so that the body of Christ may be built up. The imagery used here is of a physical body needing exercise and nourishment for growth as well as a building being constructed by many skilled craftsmen (see Eph. 2:19–22).

EPHESIANS 4:13
unity

unity in the faith. There is to be a "bond of peace" among believers because of our common faith in Christ. "Faith" refers to our common conviction about Christ and who He is.

and in the knowledge of the Son of God. There's a set standard of doctrine pertaining to Christ which cannot be compromised involving His birth, life, death, and resurrection.

maturity

become mature, attaining to the whole measure of the fullness of Christ. As defined in this verse, spiritual maturity is more than head knowledge. It is attaining an experiential knowledge of Christ in our lives. Spiritual maturity is becoming more and more like Christ in character and conduct.

EPHESIANS 4:14
immaturity

infants. Spiritually immature (see 1 Cor. 14:20; 1 Peter 2:2).

tossed. The imagery here is of a ship caught in a storm. This describes the instability of those who have not matured in their walk with Christ (see Jas. 1:6–8).

teaching ... cunning ... craftiness ... deceitful scheming. A sure mark of the immature is being led off course by distorted and heretical teaching. The teaching may sound appealing but is deadly if swallowed (see Prov. 1:30–32).

5

notes:

Session

6

What Are My Spiritual Gifts?

Prepare for the Session

	READINGS	REFLECTIVE QUESTIONS
Monday	1 Corinthians 12:1,4–7	What questions do you have about your spiritual gifts? Take those questions to God in prayer.
Tuesday	Romans 12:6–8	What do these verses tell you about the attitude God wants you to have when using your gifts and talents?
Wednesday	Ephesians 4:11–16	When have you been distracted from using your gifts as you should? What was the result?
Thursday	1 Peter 4:10–11	God provides you with the strength to use your spiritual gifts. How can you spend more time with Him on a daily basis?
Friday	1 Corinthians 12:27–30	What does it mean to you that you are part of the body of Christ?
Saturday	Romans 12:1–2	What relationship does God's will have to the gifts He has given you?
Sunday	Romans 12:3–5	How might an awareness of your gifts lead to pride? How can you stay humble?

notes:

**OUR GOALS FOR
THIS SESSION ARE:**

**⋃ In groups of 6–8,
gather people in
a horseshoe
configuration.**

**Make sure everyone
has a name tag.**

**Take time to share
information on class
parties that are coming
up as well as any
relevant church events.**

**INTRODUCE THE
ICEBREAKER ACTIVITY:
The students have
been given instructions
in their books.**

**After the Icebreaker
say something like,
"While not all-
inclusive, this
inventory gave you
a chance to think
about your gifts—
things you seem to
do well or things that
seem to be 'natural
preferences.' Today's
session will help you
understand some
specific gifts—and
encourage you to
seek God's leading
to find yours."**

**Hand out the
Prayer/Praise Report.
A sample copy is
on pages 158-159.
Have people write
down prayer requests
and praises. Then
have the prayer
coordinator collect
the report and make
copies for use during
the Caring Time.**

BIBLE STUDY
- to look at one of the spiritual gifts lists in the apostle Paul's letters
- to gain a better understanding of specific spiritual gifts

LIFE CHANGE
- to study Scripture passages on spiritual gifts
- to examine our lives for evidence of gifts
- to experiment with different kinds of ministries

Icebreaker (10-15 minutes)

Discovering Your God-Given Gifts. Here is a simple quiz to help you identify some of your spiritual gifts. It focuses on the seven gifts listed in Romans 12:6–8. For each question, choose the response that best describes you. Ignore the letters in the front of the responses until you have finished answering all the questions. Then tabulate your scores.

1. Would you consider it more loving and caring to:
   P ☐ help a person change for the better (or)
   S ☐ do something to meet a special need he or she has?

2. Are you more likely to find fulfillment in a:
   T ☐ teaching career (or)
   G ☐ business venture?

3. To form an opinion about something, would you probably:
   P ☐ go by what you feel and/or believe already (or)
   T ☐ research it until you are confident enough?

4. Would you rather encourage people to:
   G ☐ give generously to a ministry (or)
   C ☐ minister directly to those who are hurting?

5. Would you rather:
   P ☐ pray for someone (or)
   G ☐ provide for him or her?

6. In counseling people, do you:
   P ☐ tell them where they are wrong and what to do (or)
   E ☐ accept them where they are, then suggest change?

6

today's session (cont'd)

7. Would you rather:
   T ◯ train others to do a job (or)
   A ◯ delegate work to others?

8. Would you rather spend time:
   P ◯ in prayer (or)
   A ◯ organizing a Christian project?

9. Is your decision-making:
   T ◯ based on research (or)
   C ◯ difficult for you?

10. Would you rather:
    G ◯ financially assist an ongoing project (or)
    A ◯ organize the next project?

11. Would you rather participate in:
    P ◯ an intercessory prayer group (or)
    C ◯ a program to help the poor?

12. Would you rather help someone in need by:
    S ◯ doing something for him or her (or)
    G ◯ anonymously giving money?

13. Would you prefer to:
    E ◯ do individual counseling (or)
    A ◯ manage a group project?

14. Would you rather:
    S ◯ help set up for or serve a church dinner (or)
    T ◯ speak to the group after dinner?

15. If a room needed to be cleaned, would you:
    S ◯ get a broom and sweep it (or)
    A ◯ figure out who could do the job best?

16. Do you encourage people:
    E ◯ by sharing your own experiences (or)
    G ◯ by giving them practical help?

17. Would you prefer to spend your time:
    A ◯ organizing people and projects (or)
    C ◯ ministering to someone in distress?

18. Are you:
    E ◯ likely to see a problem as a challenge (or)
    C ◯ sometimes be overwhelmed by a problem?

19. Would you rather:
    S ⬭ help with a church work party (or)
    C ⬭ visit the shut-ins?

20. At a meeting, do you feel it is more important to:
    S ⬭ make sure the room is left in order (or)
    E ⬭ spend time socializing?

21. Would you prefer to:
    T ⬭ read a good book (or)
    E ⬭ be with people?

This inventory focuses on seven spiritual gifts from Romans 12:6–8.

___ Prophet/Perceiver (P)
___ Teacher (T)
___ Giver (G)
___ Server (S)
___ Administrator/Leader (A)
___ Compassion/Mercy Person (C)
___ Encourager/Exhorter (E)

Count the number of "Ps" you checked and put that number on the line next to Prophet/Perceiver. Do the same for the other letters/ gifts. When you are done, you will have an idea of what your spiritual gifts may be.[1]

6

notes:

LEARNING FROM THE BIBLE

1 CORINTHIANS 12:1

ROMANS 12:6–8

Have a member of the class, selected ahead of time, read the passages from 1 Corinthians and Romans.

Bible Study   (30-45 minutes)

The Scripture for this week:

¹*Now about spiritual gifts, brothers, I do not want you to be ignorant.*

⁶*We have different gifts, according to the grace given us. If a man's gift is prophesying, let him use it in proportion to his faith.* ⁷*If it is serving, let him serve; if it is teaching, let him teach;* ⁸*if it is encouraging, let him encourage; if it is contributing to the needs of others, let him give generously; if it is leadership, let him govern diligently; if it is showing mercy, let him do it cheerfully.*

notes:

Summarize these introductory remarks. Be sure to include the underlined information, which gives the answers to the student book questions (provided in the margin).

Why do so many Christians seem to lack the desire to serve in a ministry?

What are some reasons we should want to know our gifts?

...about today's session (5 minutes)

USING OUR GIFTS

<u>Many Christians lack the desire to serve because they don't realize their potential.</u> They have failed to understand that God has given them the tools and abilities to make a significant difference in the lives of others. In the Bible, the tools given to every believer are called spiritual gifts. Spiritual gifts are God-given abilities and skills, accompanied by the empowerment of the Holy Spirit, that help believers do the work of ministry within the church. As believers, there are several reasons we should want to know our spiritual gifts. <u>Gifts are expressions of God's love for us. Gifts give us the ability to carry out the purpose for which God created us. Gifts give each of us a sense of belonging within the body of Christ. Gifts maximize the unity and ministry of the church.</u> Today, we're going to work on discovering our spiritual gifts by studying what Paul said about specific gifts.

Remain in groups of 6–8 people, in a horseshoe configuration.

In this small-group session, students will be responding to the following questions that will help them share their stories in terms of the apostle Paul's words about spiritual gifts.

Have the students explore these questions together.

Identifying with the Story (5-7 minutes)

1. What is the best gift you've ever received for your birthday, your anniversary, or Christmas?

2. In which of the following areas would you consider yourself "ignorant"?

   ☐ auto repair
   ☐ rules of most major sports
   ☐ matching the clothes I wear
   ☐ the stock market
   ☐ setting the clock or timer on a VCR
   ☐ computers
   ☐ other:_____

3. What spiritual gifts would most qualify individuals to serve in the following positions or ministries commonly found in churches?

   BIBLE STUDY LEADER:

   EVANGELISM/OUTREACH LEADER:

   USHERS/GREETERS:

   LAY COUNSELOR:

   BENEVOLENCE MINISTRY:

   HOSPITAL VISITATION MINISTRY:

   FELLOWSHIP/SOCIAL DIRECTOR:

   BUSINESS ADMINISTRATOR:

   PASTOR/MINISTER:

6

67

today's session (15-20 minutes)

The subject of spiritual gifts has frustrated too many Christians. Some spend major amounts of energy trying to discover their spiritual gifts. Others stay confused about the topic no matter how hard they try. Most likely, the problem is that they pursue their spiritual gifts more than God, the One who gives them. A similar problem plagued the church in Corinth. Paul discovered that many of these believers wanted prominence and the approval of others. They wanted to show that they were spiritual by showing off gifts they could display. Paul confronted these sinful motives in several of his letters.

Gifts Are Manifestations of God's Grace

In three key Scriptures describing spiritual gifts, Paul identifies the giver in three different ways. In 1 Corinthians 12:7–11, the giver is the Holy Spirit. In Romans 12:3, the giver is God. In Ephesians 4:7–8, the giver is Christ. The entire Trinity is involved in gifting believers for ministry! As we talk about discovering your spiritual gifts, let's make sure we don't lose sight of our relationship with the Giver. This was Paul's emphasis in 1 Corinthians 12:4 when he used the Greek word, *charismata*, for spiritual gifts. This word means "manifestations of grace." Paul wanted the Corinthian leaders to know that their gifts were given out by the gracious act of God so He would be honored and served. God should be our focus and not jealousy or pride concerning the distribution of gifts.

God Gives Different Gifts for Different Needs

Let's begin by looking at the three different occasions where Paul provides a list of spiritual gifts. Those passages are 1 Corinthians 12:7–11,28–31; Romans 12:6–8; and Ephesians 4:11–13. We will make some observations concerning these gifts and help clear up some misunderstandings regarding these Scriptures. First, though, we need to understand why Paul's lists of spiritual gifts are different. Let's make three observations concerning these lists.

First, Paul was writing to different churches. Every church has different needs and problems. Some churches are more mature than others. This is as true today as it was in the first century. For example, in writing to the Corinthian church, Paul was writing to believers who were quarreling and distracted from serving God due to the misdirected use of gifts such as speaking in tongues. One reason Paul notes this gift is because he wants to make sure it's not a distraction in their worship services (1 Cor. 14:27–28). As Paul writes to different churches with different needs, he lists gifts they need to know about.

Second, Paul did not intend to give one comprehensive list. He didn't work from one list; God inspired him as he wrote each letter. Each of the lists are different. Some gifts are repeated and some aren't. There may not be a comprehensive gift list because God didn't want to limit the Holy Spirit's work in the church.

Third, the purpose of the gifts was to meet the needs of a particular church. Because each church experienced different needs, they were given different gifts.

God Gives a Variety of Gifts

Write several words that the leader used to characterize each of the gifts listed in Romans 12:6–8.

Prophecy:

Now, let's examine each of the ministry gifts mentioned in Romans 12:6–8. The first gift is *prophecy*. This gift enables one to use spiritual insight to communicate God's Word boldly. Prophets have the ability to see the spiritual significance of events happening around them and perceive the truth of God's Word that is needed for a particular moment.

Serving:

The second gift we see is *serving*. Those who serve have the ability to provide practical help and service to the church and others. They are able to recognize unmet and often unspoken needs in the church and meet the needs quickly and eagerly without the need to be recognized for their efforts.

Teaching:

The third gift we see is *teaching*. Those with the gift of teaching can explain the Word of God in a clear, systematic, and logical manner. Teachers have a hunger to know God's Word and present it in a way that results in the hearer experiencing life change.

Encouragement:

The fourth gift in this passage is *encouragement*. Encouragers have the ability to strengthen and motivate others. They are able to bring out the best in people and help them develop their full potential. They come alongside others to encourage the discouraged, comfort those who hurt, and spur others to good works.

Giving:

The fifth gift is *giving*. Givers earn money, manage it wisely, and give it generously. They have the ability and desire to contribute material resources to causes that help the body of Christ grow and serve.

Leadership:

The sixth gift is *administration* or *leadership*. Leaders have the ability to help others work together to accomplish the goals of the ministry. They are good organizers who can handle details, decisions, and people in an efficient, positive manner. Leaders usually don't hesitate to make an unpopular decision if it is the right decision, but they aren't dictators. Leaders simply get things done.

Mercy Giver:

The seventh gift is mercy. The compassionate mercy giver has the ability to provide emotional support to those who are suffering in the church family. They have a high sensitivity to the needs and feelings

6

today's session (cont'd)

of others. They can easily detect when someone needs empathy and compassion. They tend to be good at giving affirmation, listening, and being there for others.

Take time to study the gifts here in Romans 12 as well as the other passages. You'll gain a better understanding of how God has gifted believers for ministry.

notes:

Remain in groups of 6–8 people, in a horseshoe configuration.

In this small-group session, students will be applying the lessons of the text to their own lives through the following questions.

The students were asked (in the student book) to choose an answer for each question and explain why.

Learning from the Story (5-7 minutes)

1. If you did the Icebreaker, "Discovering Your God-Given Gifts," transfer your scores from it to the blanks below. As you do, read the descriptions of the seven types of gifts. (If you didn't do the Icebreaker, take time to do it now.)

___P = PROPHET/PERCEIVER: Truth-oriented. Forthright, out-spoken, uncompromising. Open to "inspired messages" from God, and called to pray about what is perceived. Desperately needed and potentially dangerous.

___S = SERVER: Needs-oriented. Practical. Hardworking and conscientious. Is satisfied when things get done, regardless of who gets the credit. Can be resentful when others don't serve.

___T = TEACHER. Concept-oriented. Systematic and logical. Has good insights into Scripture and makes things clear to others. Can be too intellectual.

___E = ENCOURAGER/EXHORTER. Growth-oriented. Good at setting goals and motivating others. Disciplined and single-minded. Can be demanding. Hard on self and others.

___G = GIVER: Cause-oriented. Loves to give. Able to see "big picture" and assess resources. Handles money wisely. Can be impatient with others who misuse time and/or money.

___A = ADMINISTRATOR/LEADER: Task-oriented. Organized, decisive, and thrives under pressure. Good at delegating responsibility and getting things done through others. Can be pushy.

___C = COMPASSION/MERCY GIVER: Feelings-oriented. Highly sensitive to others in need. Compassionate and affirming. Good at listening, caring, and "being present" when someone is hurting. Can get drained.

2. In which two of the gifts did you score the highest? Do you agree with that assessment, or do you see yourself with different gifts?

6

3. What effect does this study have on how you see yourself and your gifts? Will it, in any way, confirm or redirect how you function within the body of Christ?

notes:

life change lessons (5-7 minutes)

Share with the class the following thoughts on how the lessons of this text might be applied today. The answers to the student book questions (provided in the margin) are underlined unless the question requires a personal answer.

What are some steps you can take to help you discover your gifts?

List different kinds of ministries you could get involved in right now to help you determine your giftedness.

 CARING TIME
Remain in groups of 6–8 people, in a horseshoe configuration.

Hand out the Prayer/Praise Report to the entire group. Ask each subgroup to pray for the empty chair. Pray specifically for God to guide you to someone to bring next week to fill that chair.

After a sufficient time of prayer in subgroups, close in a corporate prayer. Say, "Next week we will talk about: 'Affirming Each Other's Ministry Gifts.' "

Remind participants of the daily Scripture readings and reflective questions found on page 74.

Sometimes Christians who are eager to discover their spiritual gifts look for a "magic formula" to determine their gifts. While spiritual gifts tests, inventories, and indicators can be helpful in determining areas where you may be gifted, there are also some practical things you can do to understand how God has gifted you. Here are some simple steps to help you discover your gifts.

1. <u>STUDY SCRIPTURE PASSAGES ON SPIRITUAL GIFTS</u>. There are four major passages in the New Testament which list spiritual gifts—Romans 12:6–8; Ephesians 4:11–16; 1 Corinthians 12–14; and 1 Peter 4:10–11. As you study what God's Word, the Bible, teaches about gifts, it becomes easier to see your gifts. You may also want to read books on the topic of spiritual gifts.

2. <u>EXAMINE YOUR LIFE FOR EVIDENCE OF GIFTS</u>. Look back on your Christian service and determine areas or ways you've served in the past that have been positive. Ask yourself: "What have I enjoyed doing?"; "What has God blessed?"; "Where have I made an impact on people's lives?"; "Where have I seen results?"

3. <u>EXPERIMENT WITH DIFFERENT KINDS OF MINISTRIES</u>. Maybe you haven't been involved in many ministries in the past. Start now by seeking an area of ministry that interests you. If that's not your niche, try another ministry that interests you. Eventually, one of them will feel like the right fit and you'll discover that you are good at something you enjoy doing. You're more likely to discover your spiritual gifts while you are serving than while you are sitting.

 Caring Time (15-20 minutes)

Close by praying for one another. During this time pray especially that each group member will understand how God has gifted him or her. In addition, pray for the concerns on the Prayer/Praise Report.

Conclude your prayer time by reading together Psalm 139:13–14:

> *For you created my inmost being;*
> *you knit me together in my mother's womb.*
> *I praise you because I am fearfully and wonderfully made;*
> *your works are wonderful,*
> *I know that full well.*

✝

Reference Notes

Use these notes to gain further understanding
of the text as you study on your own.

1 CORINTHIANS 12:1

Now about. Paul responds to yet another concern he has about the Corinthian church.

ROMANS 12:6
gifts

gifts. Those endowments given by God to every believer by grace (the words *grace* and *gifts* come from the same root word) to be used in God's service. The gifts listed here (and elsewhere in the New Testament) are not meant to be exhaustive or absolute since no gift list overlaps completely.

prophesying. Inspired utterances, distinguished from teaching by their immediacy and unpremeditated nature, the source of which is direct revelation by God; often directed to concrete situations, at times about the future (Acts 11:27–28), at other times about what God wants done (Acts 13:9–11); given by both men and women (Acts 21:9) and in words readily understood. Prophesying was highly valued in the New Testament church (1 Cor. 14:1).

in proportion to his faith. This could mean that prophets are to resist adding their own words to the prophecy, or it could mean that they must judge their utterances in accord with "the faith" (i.e. Christian doctrine).

ROMANS 12:7
serve and teach

serving. The special capacity to render practical service to the needy.

teaching. In contrast to the prophet (whose utterances are the direct revelation of God), the teacher relied on a study of Scripture and the teachings of Jesus to instruct others.

6

ROMANS 12:8
exercising the gifts

Paul concludes his brief discussion of spiritual gifts with this emphasis on the fact that whatever gift(s) one has, it should be exercised with enthusiasm for the good of others!

encouraging. This is supporting and assisting others to live a life of obedience to God.

contributing. The person who delights in giving away his or her finances or possessions.

leadership. Those with the special ability to guide a congregation are called upon to do so with zeal.

showing mercy. "The person whose special function is, on behalf of the congregation, to tend the sick, relieve the pain, or care for the aged or 'disabled.' "[2] Note that three of these seven gifts involve practical assistance to the needy.

[1]This exercise has been adapted from Don and Katie Fortune, *Discover Your God-Given Gifts* (Chosen Books/Baker Books, 1987). Used by permission. To order the book, the complete questionnaire, or other materials relating to spiritual gifts, contact the Fortunes at (360) 297-8878, FAX: (360) 297-8865, email: *hearttoheart@soundcom.net* or write P.O. Box 101, Kingston, WA 98346.
[2]C.E.B. Cranfield, *The International Critical Commentary: A Critical and Exegetical Commentary on the Epistle to the Romans* (Edinburgh: T & T Clark, 1979), 627.

Session

7

Affirming Each Other's Ministry Gifts

Prepare for the Session

	READINGS	REFLECTIVE QUESTIONS
Monday	Acts 4:32	How can you help the believers in your church be of "one heart and mind"?
Tuesday	Acts 4:33	Why is the resurrection of Christ our source of grace?
Wednesday	Acts 4:34–35	Are you willing to give so that there are no needy believers in your church? Who could you help this week?
Thursday	Acts 4:36–37	Would anyone change your name to "Son (or Daughter) of Encouragement"? Why or why not?
Friday	James 3:3–6	How can you discipline your tongue to speak words of encouragement, not criticism?
Saturday	Ephesians 4:29	Who do you need to "build up" or encourage today?
Sunday	Proverbs 16:24	Think about the impact of your words. How often do they help and heal?

notes:

OUR GOALS FOR THIS SESSION ARE:

♘ **In groups of 6–8, gather people in a horseshoe configuration.**

Make sure everyone has a name tag.

Take time to share information on class parties that are coming up as well as any relevant church events.

INTRODUCE THE ICEBREAKER ACTIVITY: The students have been given instructions in their books.

After the Icebreaker say something like, "There isn't a person alive who doesn't need and want to be encouraged. Let the truths of this session sink deep into your heart and be seen in your life this week. This session gives you a stepping stone to making a difference in others' lives through your words."

Hand out the Prayer/Praise Report. A sample copy is on pages 158-159. Have people write down prayer requests and praises. Then have the prayer coordinator collect the report and make copies for use during the Caring Time.

BIBLE STUDY
- to understand the power that words of encouragement can have in a person's life
- to understand the need for affirmation in confirming our gifts

LIFE CHANGE
- to intentionally look for ways to affirm and encourage others this week
- to affirm the gifts you see exhibited in the lives of others
- to encourage others to develop their gifts

Icebreaker (10-15 minutes)

Affirming Each Other. Make sure each person in your subgroup completes the following sentences about the person seated on his or her left. Then, let everyone share their completed sentences with the group.

1. In the time we have been together as a group, I have noticed that your best people skill is:

2. You are an encouragement to others in the group because:

3. In five years, you will be a successful _____ because:

7

notes:

Bible Study (30-45 minutes)

The Scripture for this week:

LEARNING FROM THE BIBLE

ACTS 4:32–37

Have one class member, selected ahead of time, read the passage from Acts.

[32]All the believers were one in heart and mind. No one claimed that any of his possessions was his own, but they shared everything they had. [33]With great power the apostles continued to testify to the resurrection of the Lord Jesus, and much grace was upon them all. [34]There were no needy persons among them. For from time to time those who owned lands or houses sold them, brought the money from the sales [35]and put it at the apostles' feet, and it was distributed to anyone as he had need.

[36]Joseph, a Levite from Cyprus, whom the apostles called Barnabas (which means Son of Encouragement), [37]sold a field he owned and brought the money and put it at the apostles' feet.

notes:

...about today's session (5 minutes)

THE DUTY TO ENCOURAGE

Summarize these introductory remarks. Be sure to include the underlined information, which gives the answers to the student book questions (provided in the margin).

What kinds of stories are usually broadcast on the local news?

Why do we as believers need words of encouragement?

What does William Barclay say is one of the highest duties of every Christian?

When you turn on the local news broadcast, most of the stories you hear concern crime or tragedy. We also receive negative information in the newspapers, on the radio, and in the mail (bills!). What people desperately desire is good news—words of encouragement. This is especially true in the church. We need to hear others say that we can make a difference with our lives. We need to know that our lives count! Where does the responsibility for that rest? It rests on each of us. William Barclay put it this way: "One of the highest duties is the duty of encouragement. ... It is easy to pour cold water on their enthusiasm; it is easy to discourage others. The world is full of discouragers. We have a Christian duty to encourage one another. Many a time, a word of praise or thanks or appreciation or cheer has kept a man on his feet."[1] Today, we'll look at the importance of encouraging one another. Specifically, we'll practice affirming one another's spiritual gifts.

🔲 Remain in groups of 6–8 people, in a horseshoe configuration.

In this small-group session, students will be responding to the following questions that will help them share their stories in terms of the apostle Paul's words about spiritual gifts.

Have the students explore these questions together.

Identifying with the Story (5-7 minutes)

1. If you met a homeless person panhandling for money, which of the following would most likely be your response?

   ☐ give some loose change
   ☐ not give anything because the person will spend it on liquor
   ☐ ask what the person needs it for
   ☐ ask how much the person needs
   ☐ tell the person about Jesus without giving money
   ☐ give the person a gospel tract instead of money
   ☐ suggest a homeless shelter nearby
   ☐ walk on the other side of the street
   ☐ make sure I don't make eye contact
   ☐ report the person to a policeman
   ☐ other:_____

2. When was the last time you accepted help from another when you had no way of helping yourself? How did it make you feel?

   ☐ thankful—I felt deep gratitude for the provision of God in my life.
   ☐ embarrassed—I felt ashamed because my need was exposed.
   ☐ obligated—I had to return the favor.
   ☐ humbled—I realized that I needed to depend on God.
   ☐ inspired—I wanted to help someone else in the same way I was helped.
   ☐ other:_____

3. Why do you think what happened in Acts 4:32–37 is not common in our churches today? What would it take to develop this kind of environment in our churches?

7

notes:

today's session (15-20 minutes)

Share with your class the following information which you may modify according to your own perspectives and teaching needs. The answers to the student book questions (provided in the margin) are underlined.

Can you think of a turning point in your life when a word of encouragement inspired you to do something you weren't sure you could do?

What advice does James 1:19 give us about the use of our words?

In James 3:3–6, what three things is the tongue compared to?

What are six steps that can help you be an encourager with your words?

As you reflect on your life, you can probably see turning points of encouragement that mark your path. Maybe a teacher told you that you would be a success some day. Maybe a friend, parent, coach, or employer breathed encouragement into your life that motivated you to try something new or to follow your dream. The great thing about encouragement is that anybody can do it. Words are important in our relationships, especially in marriage and parenting. Words can do great wonders or cause great harm. Once a word is spoken, we can never take it back. That's why James tells us to "be quick to listen, [and] slow to speak" (Jas. 1:19). In James 3:3–6, he compares the tongue to a bit in a horse's mouth, a small rudder on a big ship, and a spark that can start a raging fire. From these verses, it's obvious that words can affect our lives in significant ways.

Our Words Can Help or Hurt Others

We use words to build others up or tear them down—it's our choice. In Ephesians 4:29, Paul tells us how God expects us to use our words: "Do not let any unwholesome talk come out of your mouths, but only what is helpful for building others up according to their needs, that it may benefit those who listen."

Dennis and Barbara Rainey share a great insight into the power of words in their book, *Building Your Mate's Self-Esteem*, "Words are powerful seeds. Once planted, your words will bring forth flowers or weeds, health or disease, healing or poison. You carry a great responsibility for their use."[2] As Proverbs 16:24 tells us, words can make a huge difference in the lives of others: "Pleasant words are a honeycomb, sweet to the soul and healing to the bones."

Our Words Can Encourage Others

Here are six steps to help you become an effective encourager with your words. First, be a cheerleader for people. Those who have people on their side cheering them on are more likely to do well. Second, be intentional about encouraging others. It won't happen unless you make it a habit in your life. Third, be simple with your encouragement. Take time to write an encouraging note or speak a kind word. It may only take a moment, but your words may inspire someone for a lifetime. Fourth, be sensitive with the timing of your encouragement. Look for the right moments (Prov. 25:11)! Fifth, be transparent. One of the greatest ways to encourage people is to let them know you make mistakes. Let them know that God's free gift of forgiveness is sufficient and will be enough to help them through their difficulties. Sixth, be available for God to use you. You never know when God will bring someone your way who needs a simple word of encouragement.

78

Our Words Can Affirm Others in Their Ministries

Affirmation and encouragement are needed in our churches today to help "jump-start" individuals into ministry. People need a cheer-leader who believes in them and roots them on to victory! As we look at the early church in Acts 4:32–37, we'll focus on the power of affirmation in a man named Barnabas. In these verses, we see the church functioning as a close-knit family, meeting the needs of one another selflessly. We read of individuals selling their land and houses so they could give the money to those in need. They didn't even claim that any of their possessions were their own. This was serious ministry!

What a difference two thousand years have made! We don't see this kind of attitude and sacrifice in many of our churches today. Many may read these God-given facts and ask themselves, "What would make someone sacrifice so much to help others?" God tells us the key to this kind of heart for ministry is in verses 36–37. A man named Joseph is singled out as an example. Joseph sold a field he owned and gave the money to those in need. Why? Here are some words you need to zero in on: "whom the apostles called Barnabas (which means Son of Encouragement)." Did you see it? Apparently Joseph had such a gift of encouragement and it was so evident that the apostles affirmed Joseph's spiritual gift by calling him Barnabas, "Son of Encouragement." They affirmed his gift of encouragement by changing his name!

Who spoke words of encouragement to Joseph (Barnabas)? How did they encourage him?

Suppose you were such a great teacher that one day the leaders in your church pulled you aside and decided to begin calling you, "Master Teacher _____ (insert first name)." Yes, it would be awkward and weird in our culture today. But, the offer to change your name would obviously flatter you. More than likely, this affirmation of your spiritual gift would inspire you to be the best teacher you could be! That's the power of affirmation! What else do we know about Barnabas? This affirmation helped spur him on to more great ministries. Let's look at how God used his gift of encouragement in Acts 11:22–24: "News of this reached the ears of the church at Jerusalem, and they sent Barnabas to Antioch. When he arrived and saw the evidence of the grace of God, he was glad and encouraged them all to remain true to the Lord with all their hearts. He was a good man, full of the Holy Spirit and faith, and a great number of people were brought to the Lord." Wow! That's the power of affirmation.

How did it impact his heart for ministry?

7

All of us need to be affirmed in our spiritual gifts. We also need to make affirmation a habit in our daily lives. Let's start affirming others as we meet again with our subgroups.

Remain in groups of 6–8 people, in a horseshoe configuration.

In this small-group session, students will be applying the lessons of the text to their own lives through the following questions.

The students were asked (in the student book) to choose an answer for each question and explain why.

Learning from the Story (5-7 minutes)

1. In session 6, we examined each of the following gifts and began determining what our spiritual gifts might be. Now, take the time to affirm each other's spiritual gifts. Using the gift descriptions below as a guide, write down group members' names in the space located above the gift that you think they have. It's fine if some blanks are left blank and some blanks have more than one name. Have each person take a turn affirming the spiritual gift(s) he or she sees exhibited in the other members of the group.

Name(s) _____

PROPHET/PERCEIVER: Truth-oriented. Forthright, outspoken, uncompromising. Open to "inspired messages" from God, and called to pray about what is perceived. Desperately needed and potentially dangerous.

Name(s) _____

SERVER: Needs-oriented. Practical. Hardworking and conscientious. Is satisfied when things get done, regardless of who gets the credit. Can be resentful when others don't serve.

Name(s) _____

TEACHER. Concept-oriented. Systematic and logical. Has good insights into Scripture and makes things clear to others. Can be too intellectual.

Name(s) _____

ENCOURAGER/EXHORTER. Growth-oriented. Good at setting goals and motivating others. Disciplined and single-minded. Can be demanding. Hard on self and others.

Name(s) _____

GIVER: Cause-oriented. Loves to give. Able to see "big picture" and assess resources. Handles money wisely. Can be impatient with others who misuse time and/or money.

Name(s) _____

ADMINISTRATOR/LEADER: Task-oriented. Organized, decisive, and thrives under pressure. Good at delegating responsibility and getting things done through others. Can be pushy.

Name(s) _____

COMPASSION/MERCY GIVER: Feelings-oriented. Highly sensitive to others in need. Compassionate and affirming. Good at listening, caring, and "being present" when someone is hurting. Can get drained.

2. What effect did this exercise have on the way you see yourself and your gifts? Will it, in any way, confirm or redirect the way you function within the body of Christ?

n<u>otes</u>:

life change lessons (5-7 minutes)

Serving God can sometimes produce feelings of inadequacy and loneliness. We all need encouragement to help us "not grow weary in doing good" (2 Thess. 3:13b). Here are some practical ways you can begin encouraging and affirming others:

1. <u>INTENTIONALLY LOOK FOR WAYS TO AFFIRM AND ENCOURAGE OTHERS THIS WEEK</u>. Sometimes we miss the obvious about ourselves because of a poor self-image, lack of confidence, or "busyness." The easiest thing to do is be critical of someone's faults, failures, and weaknesses. That seems to come natural to us. We need to be aware of our words. We can help people believe in themselves or destroy them.

2. <u>AFFIRM THE GIFTS YOU SEE EXHIBITED IN THE LIVES OF OTHERS</u>. We also need to continually encourage one another's ministry strengths. When someone does a good job teaching a lesson, let the person know. When someone gives you an encouraging word, tell the person how much it means. When someone shows exceptional skill in leading a group toward a goal, let the person know. The writer of Hebrews tells us to "consider how we may spur one another on toward love and good deeds" (Heb. 10:24). There's nothing better than an encouraging word to inspire us into action!

life change lessons (cont'd)

What are some ways you can encourage a potential leader you know to develop his or her gifts?

3. <u>ENCOURAGE OTHERS TO DEVELOP THEIR GIFTS</u>. You can also be an encouragement to others by providing tapes or books to help them develop their particular gift or strength. You could also invite them to the next leadership training that the church sponsors. A practical way to encourage another person in ministry is to personally mentor him or her in the ministry you are currently involved with. We will look at mentoring more closely in session 11.

notes:

CARING TIME
Remain in groups of 6–8 people, in a horseshoe configuration.

Hand out the Prayer/Praise Report to the entire group. Ask each subgroup to pray for the empty chair. Pray specifically for God to guide you to someone to bring next week to fill that chair.

After a sufficient time of prayer in subgroups, close in a corporate prayer. Say, "Next week we will talk about: 'Journaling My Life Experiences.' "

Remind participants of the daily Scripture readings and reflective questions found on page 84.

 Caring Time (15-20 minutes)

Close by praying for one another. During this time, ask God to give you the ability to encourage others. Pray that God would continue to develop the gifts that have been affirmed in the lives of class members today. Also, use the Prayer/Praise Report and pray for the requests listed.

notes:

✝

Reference Notes

Use these notes to gain further understanding
of the text as you study on your own.

ACTS 4:32
share freely

Compare with Acts 2:44–45. This sharing was done freely as an expression of love for one another; it may be intended as another sign of the Spirit at work (Acts 4:31).

ACTS 4:33
grace

much grace was upon them all. That is, upon all the believers, not just the apostles. The mutual caring and help (vv. 34–35) was an indication of God's grace in their midst.

ACTS 4:34
none in need

no needy persons among them. While this was the ideal for Old Testament Israel (Deut. 15:4), the generosity of the Christians allowed it to be experienced (see Luke 12:32–34; 18:18–30; 19:1–10). One of Paul's major expressions of Gentile solidarity with Jewish Christians was taking up a collection among the Gentile churches to be given to the needy in Jerusalem (Acts 11:28–30; 24:17; Rom. 15:26; 1 Cor. 16:1–3; 2 Cor. 8–9; Gal. 2:10).

ACTS 4:35
a transfer

put it at the apostles' feet. A way of referring to the transfer of the rights of ownership much as we might say two people "shook hands on the deal" or signed papers. The apostles were given the responsibility of distributing the resources so that all the needs of the believers were met.

notes:

7

[1] William Barclay, "The Letters to the Hebrews," *The Daily Study Bible* (Edinburgh: The Saint Andrews Press, 1955), 137–138.
[2] Dennis and Barbara Rainey, *Building Your Mate's Self-Esteem* (Nashville, TN: Thomas Nelson Publishers, 1993), 104.

Session

8

Journaling
My Life Experiences

Prepare for the Session

	READINGS	REFLECTIVE QUESTIONS
Monday	2 Corinthians 11:23–29	What qualifications for service would you list on your spiritual resumé?
Tuesday	Philippians 1:9–14	How can your actions bring glory and praise to God this week?
Wednesday	Romans 8:28	Do you believe that everything that has happened to you has been for your good? Why or why not?
Thursday	James 1:2–4	How would you describe your attitude toward trials?
Friday	2 Corinthians 1:3–4	When has God comforted you in a time of trial?
Saturday	2 Corinthians 5:18–20	To whom do you need to bring a "message of reconciliation"?
Sunday	Philippians 3:1–11	As you look back on your life, how has every experience enabled you to know and serve Christ better?

notes:

OUR GOALS FOR THIS SESSION ARE:

♆ **In groups of 6–8, gather people in a horseshoe configuration.**

Make sure everyone has a name tag.

Take time to share information on class parties that are coming up as well as any relevant church events.

INTRODUCE THE ICEBREAKER ACTIVITY: The students have been given instructions in their books.

After the Icebreaker say something like, "In today's session, we'll look at how God has been shaping you for ministry through the experiences in your life."

Hand out the Prayer/Praise Report. A sample copy is on pages 158-159. Have people write down prayer requests and praises. Then have the prayer coordinator collect the report and make copies for use during the Caring Time.

✝ BIBLE STUDY

- to realize that God never wastes a hurt
- to learn how our experiences help shape our ability to minister to others
- to understand that God wants to use our life experiences in a current ministry

LIFE CHANGE

- to minister to someone who is going through a trial or problem we've already been through
- to become part of a ministry that can benefit from our life experiences
- to share our salvation experiences with another person this week

Icebreaker (10-15 minutes)

Adventure Inventory. Which of the following adventures have you already experienced and which one would you most like to experience in your lifetime?

- ☐ skydive out of an airplane
- ☐ go on an African safari
- ☐ have a speaking part in a movie
- ☐ drive a race car at 180 mph
- ☐ bungee jump
- ☐ run with the bulls in Spain
- ☐ hang glide over the Grand Canyon
- ☐ scuba dive in the Caribbean
- ☐ other:_____

8

notes:

Bible Study   (30-45 minutes)

**2 CORINTHIANS
11:23–29**

**Select two members
of the class ahead of
time. Have one read
the passage in
2 Corinthians;
then have the other
read the passages
in Philippians
and Romans.**

The Scripture for this week:

[23]I have worked much harder, been in prison more frequently, been flogged more severely, and been exposed to death again and again. [24]Five times I received from the Jews the forty lashes minus one. [25]Three times I was beaten with rods, once I was stoned, three times I was shipwrecked, I spent a night and a day in the open sea, [26]I have been constantly on the move. I have been in danger from rivers, in danger from bandits, in danger from my own countrymen, in danger from Gentiles; in danger in the city, in danger in the country, in danger at sea; and in danger from false brothers. [27]I have labored and toiled and have often gone without sleep; I have known hunger and thirst and have often gone without food; I have been cold and naked. [28]Besides everything else, I face daily the pressure of my concern for all the churches. [29]Who is weak, and I do not feel weak? Who is led into sin, and I do not inwardly burn?"

PHILIPPIANS 1:12

[12]I want you to know, brothers, that what has happened to me has really served to advance the gospel.

ROMANS 8:28

[28]We know that in all things God works for the good of those who love him, who have been called according to his purpose.

notes:

Summarize these introductory remarks. Be sure to include the underlined information, which gives the answers to the student book questions (provided in the margin).

Why is job experience important to a would-be employer?

What is God's plan for your life experiences?

...about today's session (5 minutes)

EXPERIENCE REQUIRED

You've probably heard this statement before: "Experience isn't anything. It's the only thing!" In the workplace, heavy emphasis is placed on a person's experience. When someone is under consideration for a raise or promotion, often that person's experience is a significant factor. Certainly in job interviews, potential candidates are asked about their qualifications—primarily their experiences that will benefit their would-be employer. Companies look for individuals who don't need much training or preparation time so that results come sooner rather than later. The importance of experience is seen in professional sports also. For instance, when the media picks baseball teams that should be favorites to make the play-offs and World Series, they often highlight the "veteran" team members, especially those who have play-off experience. Employers and team owners understand the value of experience in the employees they pursue.

Lack of experience usually doesn't disqualify you from entering a particular occupational field because, after all, everyone's got to start somewhere. But the most important and higher paying positions tend to be given to those whose experience will benefit the organization most. The goal is to place those with certain educational and job experiences in positions that line up with those experiences. For employers, the bottom line is to find the right person for the job. That is God's plan for us—to make us the right person for the job. In today's session, we'll see how God has been using your life experiences to mold and shape you into the right person for a job He has designed just for you.

8

notes:

87

Remain in groups of 6–8 people, in a horseshoe configuration.

In this small-group session, students will be responding to the following questions that will help them share their stories in terms of Paul's words about his life experiences.

Have the students explore these questions together.

Identifying with the Story (5-7 minutes)

1. The list of painful experiences encountered by the apostle Paul in 2 Corinthians 11:23–29 would surely challenge any Christian's commitment today. Order the following experiences from 1–12 with 1 being the experience you think would most challenge your commitment and faith in Christ and 12 representing the experience you think would least challenge your faith.

   _____ frequent imprisonments
   _____ severe beating on 3 different occasions
   _____ 39 lashes on 5 different occasions
   _____ have rocks thrown at you by a crowd
   _____ be shipwrecked 3 times
   _____ travel down treacherous rivers
   _____ be a victim of robbery and assault
   _____ be physically threatened by those closest to you
   _____ be adrift on roaring seas in severe storms
   _____ hard labor during the day and sleepless nights on a regular basis
   _____ no food or water for long periods of time
   _____ extended period of time in cold weather with no clothing

2. If, in the midst of serving God, you encountered the same dangers, situations, labors, and hardships that Paul did, which of the following would probably resemble your attitude?

   ☐ "Take this job and shove it."
   ☐ "Never surrender, never say die."
   ☐ "Why me, God?"
   ☐ "God, I hope you know what you're doing."
   ☐ "I know this is all part of God's plan, so I'm not going to question God."
   ☐ "I am weak but you (God) are strong."
   ☐ Other:_____

3. How did Paul's experiences serve to advance the gospel? How do you think God is using your experiences to advance the gospel?

notes:

Share with your class the following information which you may modify according to your own perspectives and teaching needs. The answers to the student book questions (provided in the margin) are underlined.

What must a Christian do when faced with heartache, pain, or adversity?

What are three truths we can learn from the apostle Paul regarding our past experiences?

today's session (15-20 minutes)

Most of us have a mental picture or vision of what we think our lives will look like in the future. This preferred future most likely doesn't include heartache, pain, or adversity. So when unexpected situations arise, we are faced with a choice: We can get bitter toward God or we can choose to get better. The old saying goes, "I can't help it if a bird flies over my head, but I can choose whether or not it makes a nest in my hair." It's alright, even healthy, to ask God, "Why?" But, it's unhealthy to continue asking the question if we are growing distant from God. God wants us to shift from asking, "Why, God?" to "What, God, are you showing me?" The answer to the "What?" question may also be cloudy for awhile. <u>During those times, we must trust God's heart even when we can't trace His hand</u>. All of us experience adversity in our lives. If we will let Him, God will shape us through those experiences and use them (and us) for His purposes. Today, we'll gain some insight from the apostle Paul concerning the way God wants to use our past experiences for the purpose of ministry.

God Never Wastes a Hurt

If there was ever anyone who had a hard time of it, it was the apostle Paul. In 2 Corinthians 11:23–27, we get a look into Paul's own journal and see many of his painful experiences. Just look at the adversity he faced: "Worked much harder ... prison more frequently ... flogged more severely ... exposed to death again and again ... forty lashes minus one ... beaten with rods ... stoned ... shipwrecked ... open sea ... constantly on the move ... in danger from rivers, in danger from bandits, in danger from my own countrymen, in danger from Gentiles; in danger in the city, in danger in the country, in danger at sea; in danger from false brothers ... labored ... toiled ... often gone without sleep ... hunger ... thirst ... often gone without food ... cold ... naked."

today's session (cont'd)

Most of us appreciate Paul's dedication and work for the Lord, but deep inside we are glad it was he who had to endure such unbelievable adversity and not us! Hurtful experiences tend to cloud our view of God and His goodness. Some examples of how we respond to God include: running from God, blaming God, getting angry at God, and ignoring God. If a tragedy happens to someone around the world, we're quick to offer prayer or financial aid. Our response is full of faith as we respond, "God will help you through this. He'll use it for His glory. I'll keep praying for you." However, when the hurt becomes personal, our response tends to change. The hurt clouds our view of God's motives.

We tend to look at adversity with a _____.

God looks at our adversity with a _____.

It is then that we need to look at the situation the way God sees things. We tend to look at adversity with a <u>microscope</u>. God looks at our adversity with a <u>wide-angle telescope</u>. He sees the big picture and understands how our experiences are working to mature us and prepare us to serve Him. In Romans 8:28, we see how Paul viewed his experiences with godly vision: "We know that in all things God works for the good of those who love him, who have been called according to his purpose." God works everything, good and bad, pleasant and painful, for our good and His purpose. In Isaiah 38:17, King Hezekiah gained great insight from an illness that brought him close to death: "Surely it was for my benefit that I suffered such anguish."

God never wastes a hurtful experience in our lives. God uses those experiences to mature us in our faith. In James 1:2–4, we see how God uses trials for our spiritual development: "Consider it pure joy, my brothers, whenever you face trials of many kinds, because you know that the testing of your faith develops perseverance. Perseverance must finish its work so that you may be mature and complete, not lacking anything." Not only does God use our hurts to develop us spiritually, but He uses our hurts to increase our capacity to minister to others.

Our Experiences Help Shape Our Ability to Minister to Others

In 2 Corinthians 1:3–4, Paul describes how God uses our painful experiences to increase our ability to minister to others: "Praise be to the God and Father of our Lord Jesus Christ, the Father of compassion and the God of all comfort, who comforts us in all our troubles, so that we can comfort those in any trouble with the comfort we ourselves have received from God." God also used Paul's previous educational experiences in shaping his ministry. In Acts 22:3, Paul states: "Under Gamaliel, I was thoroughly trained in the law of our fathers." Paul's

spiritual experiences also contributed to his development. Paul's conversion on the Damascus Road (Acts 9:1–19) and his three years maturing in Arabia (Gal. 1:17) are examples of spiritual experiences that marked his life. Paul's wide range of ministry experiences are recorded in the book of Acts. Why does God place such great emphasis on experiences in developing our ability to minister? <u>The greatest depth of learning doesn't come by listening or watching; it occurs by doing</u>. While we typically forget 95 percent of what we hear after 72 hours, our experiences intensify the depth and longevity of our learning. Based on your life experiences, what ministry do you think God is preparing you for?

How does the greatest depth of learning occur?

God Wants to Use Your Life Experiences in a Current Ministry

Our capacity for ministry increases as God matures us through the various experiences of life. It's up to us to let others benefit from what we've learned. Paul knew that his experiences contributed to the advancement of God's work in the world through Jesus Christ. In Philippians 1:12, Paul saw his prison detainment from God's perspective. "Now I want you to know, brothers, that what has happened to me has really served to advance the gospel." We must not overlook our past experiences as a major factor in determining the ministry God has planned for us. We must ask the question: "What ministry could benefit most from my educational, ministry, spiritual, and painful experiences?"

notes:

8

◡ Remain in groups of 6–8 people, in a horseshoe configuration.

In this small-group session, students will be applying the lessons of the text to their own lives through the following questions.

The students were asked (in the student book) to choose an answer for each question and explain why.

Learning from the Story (5-7 minutes)

Spend a few minutes journaling at least one life experience in each of the following four areas. Take turns sharing one area of experience with the group.

1. My Spiritual Experiences (Briefly describe your transformation story [how you became a Christian], times you've trusted God, etc.)

2. My Painful Experiences (List some trials or problems you could use to encourage a fellow Christian going through a similar situation.)

3. My Educational Experiences (List schools you attended, subjects you enjoyed, major seminars or training you've benefited from, books you've read that have changed you, etc.)

4. My Ministry Experiences (Name church or parachurch organizations you've served including areas and length of service.)

notes:

life change lessons (5-7 minutes)

Too often Christians fall into the trap of thinking that for God to use them greatly, they must attend extra training and seminars, read a large number of books, have a certain gift or possess a particular skill. Unfortunately, many well-intentioned Christians forget about the "school of hard knocks" that God has brought them through over the years. God is ready to use our painful experiences along with our education, ministry, and spiritual experiences in ministry right now! Here are some ways you can begin to make the most of the experiences God has allowed you to encounter:

What are three ways to make the most of the experiences God has allowed you to encounter?

1. MINISTER TO SOMEONE WHO IS GOING THROUGH A TRIAL OR PROBLEM THAT YOU'VE ALREADY BEEN THROUGH. You might be hesitant to share your painful experiences with others. Maybe you're thinking, "I'm scared of what they might think of me," or "I don't think they would want to hear my story." You would be surprised at how helpful you could be to someone who is hurting if you would be open and let God use you. Make sure you use sensitivity and appropriate timing if you feel led to offer assistance. Most of us have had the comforting experience of people who came alongside us during difficult times. When they can relate to what you're going through because they've already traveled down the road you're traveling, their ability to comfort multiplies. Never underestimate God's ability to use the painful experiences of your life to bring peace and assurance to the life of another.

2. BECOME PART OF A MINISTRY THAT CAN BENEFIT FROM YOUR LIFE EXPERIENCES. Keep journaling your life experiences and examining them closely for a ministry theme that God may be establishing in your life. Let others read the various experiences you wrote a few minutes ago and get their input as to an area of ministry that could be best suited for you. Sometimes others can see the forest while we're staring at the trees. Just think, God has been weaving the experiences of your life through His hand, designing you for a ministry that will honor Him.

What is the greatest experience you can share with another person?

3. SHARE YOUR TRANSFORMATION STORY, HOW YOU BECAME A CHRISTIAN, WITH ANOTHER PERSON THIS WEEK. The greatest experience you can share with another person is your salvation experience. This is one ministry that God has called every believer to. In 2 Corinthians 5:18–20, Paul explains our responsibility: "All this is from God, who reconciled us to himself through Christ and gave us the ministry of reconciliation: that God was reconciling the world to himself in Christ, not counting men's sins against them. And he has committed to us the message of reconciliation.

8

life change lessons (cont'd)

We are therefore Christ's ambassador, as though God were making his appeal through us." Accepting Christ as Savior ... being forgiven of your sins ... this reconciliation which takes place when we humble ourselves before God is the most important experience you can ever share.

notes:

Caring Time   (15-20 minutes)

Has anyone in your group experienced a particularly painful event that is still causing unforgiveness, stress, bitterness, or despair? Have a time of prayer for those who feel free enough to share their hurts. Ask God to heal their wounds. Make sure each person in the group is encouraged by the fact that "God never wastes a hurt." In addition, pray for the concerns on the Prayer/Praise Report.

CARING TIME
Remain in groups of 6–8 people, in a horseshoe configuration.

Hand out the Prayer/ Praise Report to the entire group. Ask each subgroup to pray for the empty chair. Pray specifically for God to guide you to someone to bring next week to fill that chair.

After a sufficient time of prayer in subgroups, close in a corporate prayer. Say, "Next week we will talk about: 'Putting It All Together.' "

Remind participants of the daily Scripture readings and reflective questions found on page 96.

notes:

BIBLE STUDY NOTES

Reference Notes

Use these notes to gain further understanding
of the text as you study on your own.

2 CORINTHIANS 11:23
death

exposed to death again and again. From Paul's list here, it's apparent that Luke's description of Paul's ministry in the book of Acts was not a complete account of Paul's experiences.

**2 CORINTHIANS
11:24–25**
pain

lashes ... rods. The Jews administered the 39 lashes five different times. This was potentially a deadly punishment. According to Jewish law, the person who delivered the scourging could not be held responsible for the victim's death. The Roman authorities also beat Paul with rods even though this was illegal since Paul was a Roman citizen (see Acts 16:37).

2 CORINTHIANS 11:25
shipwreck

stoned. This was a traditional manner of Jewish execution; the rocks were meant to kill Paul (see Acts 14:19).

shipwrecked. Although only one shipwreck account is mentioned in Acts, others most likely took place during other voyages mentioned in Acts.

a night and a day in the open sea. Most likely, this was due to one of the shipwrecks he mentions.

2 CORINTHIANS 11:26
flood

in danger. Paul's repeated mention of being "in danger" tells us that his life was at stake almost constantly.

rivers. Most likely, this refers to flooding rivers. Due to waters coming down from Lebanon, the road between Jerusalem and Antioch was often flooded and dangerous. This was a road that Paul traveled frequently.

PHILIPPIANS 1:12
testimony

what has happened to me. Paul is referring to being held in prison (see Phil. 1:13).

advance the gospel. As is often the case, attempts to stifle the spread of the gospel only serve to fan its flames. Paul wanted the believers at Philippi to know that there are no accidents with God.

ROMANS 8:28
called

the good. The good that is mentioned here refers to our becoming more Christlike in character and conduct (see Rom. 8:29).

called. This refers to God's calling and sovereign work in a person's life that achieves God's purposes (Rom. 1:6; 8:30). This calling produces a love for God through the work of the Holy Spirit (Rom. 5:5; 1 John 4:19).

8

notes:

Session

9

Putting It All Together

Prepare for the Session

	READINGS	REFLECTIVE QUESTIONS
Monday	Matthew 13:44	How willing are you to give up everything for God?
Tuesday	1 Corinthians 9:16	What are you "compelled" to do for God?
Wednesday	Romans 1:11–17	Have you ever been ashamed of being a Christian?
Thursday	Romans 15:17,20	What is your spiritual ambition?
Friday	Colossians 3:23–24	How often do you find yourself working to please people rather than the Lord?
Saturday	Galatians 4:4–7	How does it make you feel to know you can call the God of the universe, "Father"?
Sunday	2 Timothy 4:7	How are you doing at fighting the "good fight"?

notes:

OUR GOALS FOR THIS SESSION ARE:

⊍ **In groups of 6–8, gather people in a horseshoe configuration.**

Make sure everyone has a name tag.

Take time to share information on class parties that are coming up as well as any relevant church events.

INTRODUCE THE ICEBREAKER ACTIVITY: The students have been given instructions in their books.

After the Icebreaker say something like, "Your favorite activities probably brought you great happiness. Today's session will help you see the joy in serving God."

Hand out the Prayer/Praise Report. A sample copy is on pages 158-159. Have people write down prayer requests and praises. Then have the prayer coordinator collect the report and make copies for use during the Caring Time.

✝

BIBLE STUDY
· to realize the importance of serving with joy
· to learn that passionate people get results
· to understand that God wants us to do His work with all of our passion and commitment

LIFE CHANGE
· to make an assessment of the things we enjoy doing
· to learn about and try different areas of service
· to start serving in spite of our fears

 Icebreaker (10-15 minutes)

Favorite Activities. As a child, which of the following things did you enjoy doing the most? Which did you enjoy doing the least? Discuss how different your group responses are.

☐ homework
☐ family vacation
☐ playing with toys inside
☐ going to school
☐ household chores
☐ reading
☐ going to the movies
☐ camping
☐ playing organized sports
☐ taking music lessons
☐ other:_____

9

notes:

Bible Study (30-45 minutes)

The Scripture for this week:

MATTHEW 13:44

⁴⁴*The kingdom of heaven is like treasure hidden in a field. When a man found it, he hid it again, and then in his joy went and sold all he had and bought that field.*

1 CORINTHIANS 9:16

¹⁶*When I preach the gospel, I cannot boast, for I am compelled to preach. Woe to me if I do not preach the gospel!*

ROMANS 1:15

¹⁵*That is why I am so eager to preach the gospel also to you who are at Rome.*

ROMANS 15:20

²⁰*It has always been my ambition to preach the gospel where Christ was not known, so that I would not be building on someone else's foundation.*

COLOSSIANS 3:23–24

Ask for volunteers to read these passages out loud.

²³*Whatever you do, work at it with all your heart, as working for the Lord, not for men,* ²⁴*since you know that you will receive an inheritance from the Lord as a reward. It is the Lord Christ you are serving.*

notes:

...about today's session (5 minutes)

FOLLOW YOUR HEART

Summarize these introductory remarks. Be sure to include the underlined information, which gives the answers to the student book questions (provided in the margin).

Throughout this study we have focused on understanding the way God has been shaping and molding us for ministry. We have looked at personality, abilities, spiritual gifts, and experiences. Today, we are going to look at the glue that joins all of these pieces together!

What motive for doing ministry will only produce temporary results?

Many well-meaning Christians will go to great lengths to find out how they fit into a specific ministry. They will take all kinds of assessment tests, spiritual gift inventories, personality profiles, etc. The problem is they fail to follow their "heart." Serving out of obligation or duty will only last temporarily. There must be something deeper and greater to sustain our fervor for ministry. The greatest motivation for ministry comes from a passion in our hearts that God has placed there. We must ask ourselves, "What is it that stirs our emotions?" Have you noticed that some of you are more passionate and feel more deeply about some things than others? Because God designed each of us differently, those activities, subjects, and needs that you feel strongly about may not bring the same excitement and fervor to the person sitting next to you. God has placed those inborn interests in your life for a reason. God wants you to understand that this is an important key in understanding how He has designed you. Not only do you need to discover "how" God has shaped and molded you for ministry, but you also need to consider "what" you love to do. Today, you will be challenged to identify those things you're good at and are motivated to do.

Why is discovering what you love to do an important part of finding your place in ministry?

notes:

9

99

Remain in groups of 6–8 people, in a horseshoe configuration.

In this small-group session, students will be responding to the following questions that will help them share their stories in terms of the parable of the hidden treasure and Paul's words about spiritual ambition.

Have the students explore these questions together.

Identifying with the Story (5-7 minutes)

1. In the parable of the hidden treasure in Matthew 13:44, a man found a treasure hidden in a field. Which of the following items would most likely be found hidden under the cushions of a sofa or chair in your home?

   ☐ popcorn   ☐ potato chips
   ☐ coins   ☐ small child's toy
   ☐ remote control   ☐ pen or pencil
   ☐ keys   ☐ fork

2. Match the biblical characters with their passion:

   ___ Moses   a. Rebuild a wall around Jerusalem
   ___ David   b. Preach the gospel to the Gentiles
   ___ Noah   c. Build a temple
   ___ Joshua   d. Build an ark
   ___ Nehemiah   e. Build a people for God through his
                         descendants
   ___ Paul   f. Bring down the walls around Jericho
   ___ Abraham   g. Release his people from Egyptian slavery

3. What was your first job? Of the jobs that you've previously held, what is the one you most enjoyed? Why?

notes:

today's session (15-20 minutes)

What is a major difference between Christianity and other religions?

What are three things we should know about serving out of our heart's desire?

Christianity is lived from the inside out. Other religions tend to focus on external rules and regulations where people try to reach God through their own efforts. Because Christianity is lived in the context of an intimate relationship with Christ, we are to serve in the power of the Holy Spirit who is at work in our hearts. Galatians 4:6 tells us, "Because you are sons, God sent the Spirit of his Son into our hearts, the Spirit who calls out, 'Abba, Father.' " This intimate relationship with God is the way God desires to work in us. Philippians 2:13 says, "For it is God who works in you to will and to act according to his good purpose." Therefore, the power and strength for our ministry must come from the desires that the Holy Spirit generates in our hearts. In Colossians 1:28–29, Paul explained it this way: "We proclaim him, admonishing and teaching everyone with all wisdom, so that we may present everyone perfect in Christ. To this end I labor, struggling with all his energy, which so powerfully works in me." Here are some things to keep in mind as we consider serving out of our heart's desire.

Our Ministry Will Last Only If We Serve with Joy

The best jobs are the ones where you never have to look at the clock or wonder when the end of the work day will come. Sadly, many people in our society work in jobs they hate. Their only motivation is the paycheck and a supervisor looking over their shoulder. God doesn't want us to serve with this type of mentality. In fact, God wants us to serve in a ministry that fulfills our deepest longings and desires. He wants us to serve with enthusiasm. Rewards and supervision become distant considerations. In Matthew 13:44, Jesus told a parable describing the kind of joy that should accompany giving up our lives to serve Him: "The kingdom of heaven is like treasure hidden in a field. When a man found it, he hid it again, and then in his joy went and sold all he had and bought that field." God never meant actions that advance His kingdom to be drudgery for believers. One of the keys to a sustained ministry is doing what you love to do. Most likely, previous attempts at ministry that fizzled out probably ended when you realized that it wasn't something you loved to do. It didn't match your ambitions, dreams, interests, and passions. God wants us to serve in a ministry that naturally motivates us because it involves a group or subject for which we have a passion.

Passionate People Get Results

One of the results of serving in an area you have a heart for is that you are persistent and won't stop until you get the job done. When you unleash your passion, your life becomes more focused. When you give your life to a cause, idea, group, or task, you no longer

9

today's session (cont'd)

settle for doing things halfway. Passionate people get things done! They produce results. In the Bible, we could think of many individuals who had a God-given passion and made a difference. For example, the apostle Paul could definitely be described as an individual who was passionate about his ministry. In 1 Corinthians 9:16 Paul wrote, "Yet when I preach the gospel, I cannot boast, for I am compelled to preach. Woe to me if I do not preach the gospel!" In Romans 1:15, Paul wrote, "That is why I am so eager to preach the gospel also to you who are at Rome." In Romans 15:20, Paul wrote, "It has always been my ambition to preach the gospel where Christ was not known, so that I would not be building on someone else's foundation." Paul's ministry came from a God-given passion in his heart. The book of Acts chronicles the results of his ministry. In 2 Timothy 4:7, Paul described his life of ministry like this, "I have fought the good fight, I have finished the race, I have kept the faith." He could say this because he pursued the internal passion that God had placed in his heart. History holds many examples of individuals who made a great impact because they acted out of the passion in their hearts. What passion has God placed in your heart?

God Wants Us to Minister with All Our Hearts

Many Christians are satisfied with serving God inside the boat instead of stepping out on the water. They'd rather play it safe and not have to place everything in God's hands. But as God's children, we're called to minister and serve with all our hearts. This means we'll have to take risks for God. But it is the risk-takers who get to experience the power of God far beyond anything the "boat huggers" will ever experience. In Colossians 3:23–24, Paul gives this instruction: "Whatever you do, work at it with all your heart, as working for the Lord, not for men, since you know that you will receive an inheritance from the Lord as a reward. It is the Lord Christ you are serving." We must place our interests, passions, ambitions, and dreams at His feet and allow God to act on them. If we're not careful, we can begin to pursue the selfish longings of our hearts. What are the right motives? Compassion for people and a hunger for God!

What are the right motives for serving in a ministry?

What is the key to serving God with all our hearts?

The key to serving God with all our hearts is investing in our relationship with Him. Psalm 37:4 shows us the necessity of finding our satisfaction in God: "Delight yourself in the Lord and he will give you the desires of your heart." As we spend time getting to know God, we will become concerned about the things He is concerned about and passionate about the things He is passionate about. In that personal relationship with God, He sparks in each of us a vision for ministry. He wants us to pursue that ministry with all our hearts. Let's not be comfortable in the boat. Step out and pursue the desires that God has placed in your heart for His glory!

Remain in groups
of 6–8 people, in
a horseshoe
configuration.

In this small-group
session, students will
be applying the lessons
of the text to their
own lives through the
following questions.

The students were
asked (in the student
book) to choose an
answer for each
question and
explain why.

Learning from the Story (5-7 minutes)

1. Which of the following types of activities do you love to do the most?

   ☐ acquire things
   ☐ influence others
   ☐ repair things
   ☐ design/develop ideas or processes
   ☐ lead or be in charge
   ☐ help/assist others
   ☐ organize/bring order out of chaos
   ☐ overcome injustices
   ☐ try new things or test new concepts
   ☐ improve things someone else has started
   ☐ perform for others (sing, speak, etc.)
   ☐ other:_____

2. Think of your favorite hobby. Now, think of a way you could turn that hobby into a ministry. What would you name it? Who would be your target audience?

3. What is one vision or dream for God that you haven't told anyone about? How much risk is involved on your part? Is this something you could pursue with all your heart? What resources would be required to get your vision started?

4. Complete the following sentences as they relate to what you've discovered about yourself in this study on spiritual passions.

   My personality could best be described as:

   My greatest abilities and talents are:

   My primary spiritual gifts are:

   My life experiences have equipped me to help others by:

   My heart's desire for ministry is to:

9

life change lessons (5-7 minutes)

Share with the class the following thoughts on how the lessons of this text might be applied today. The answers to the student book questions (provided in the margin) are underlined unless the question requires a personal answer.

What are three steps you can take to begin living out your heart's desire in ministry?

What fears can keep Christians from pursuing the dream God has put in their hearts?

What fears are keeping you from moving ahead with your ministry? How can you overcome your fears?

1. <u>MAKE AN ASSESSMENT OF THE THINGS YOU ENJOY DOING</u>. Through the years, you've more than likely accomplished some things that have given you a sense of satisfaction. Take some time to write out some of the accomplishments and activities you enjoyed as a child, as a teen, in your college years, etc. See if you can find a common motivational thread in your list. Look for recurring phrases and themes. Ask yourself what you're really good at and what you've been the most successful at. Think about the things you really enjoy doing. This could include things you do as a hobby, at work, at church, etc.

2. <u>LEARN ABOUT AND TRY DIFFERENT TYPES OF SERVICE</u>. We may not know that we enjoy a particular type of work or area of ministry until we attempt different ones. Explore your options; don't lock yourself into one particular ministry. Try several areas of work and find one that fits you. There are urgent needs all around us. Just jump in and start serving. Even if you don't get to experience other ministries, you can talk to people who are doing different types of ministries to see if you have the same heart they do. Spend time around other people who have similar passions as you and learn all you can.

3. <u>START SERVING IN SPITE OF YOUR FEARS</u>. Too many Christians live unfulfilled lives because they don't pursue the dream or passion God has put in their hearts. <u>People worry about what others will think</u>. <u>They are scared of failure</u>. <u>They don't have all the answers</u>. God wants us to move ahead with courage in spite of our fears. When God births a deep desire in your heart, a vision to accomplish something great for His kingdom, He will always equip you with what you need. <u>You can overcome your fears through faith in God's ability to empower you for ministry (Josh. 1:9; Phil. 2:13)</u>. Just ask yourself, "What would I attempt for God if I knew it wouldn't fail?"

⊌ CARING TIME
Remain in groups of 6–8 people, in a horseshoe configuration.

Hand out the Prayer/ Praise Report to the entire group. Ask each subgroup to pray for the empty chair. Pray specifically for God to guide you to someone to bring next week to fill that chair.

After a sufficient time of prayer in subgroups, close in a corporate prayer. Say, "Next week we will talk about: 'Finding My Ministry.'"

Caring Time (15-20 minutes)

Use this time to pray for one another and the dreams that have been shared. Pray that God will give group members the courage to follow through on the desires of their hearts. Also, use the Prayer/Praise Report and pray for the concerns listed.

CARING TIME (cont'd)

Remind participants of the daily Scripture readings and reflective questions found on page 106.

notes:

BIBLE STUDY NOTES

MATTHEW 13:44
treasure

1 CORINTHIANS 9:16
burden

ROMANS 1:15
be patient

ROMANS 15:20
ambition

COLOSSIANS 3:23–24
servants of God

Reference Notes

Use these notes to gain further understanding
of the text as you study on your own.

treasure hidden in a field. Hiding treasure in the ground was common in ancient times because banks didn't exist (although there were "bankers"—see Matthew 25:27). In this parable, Jesus did not mean that you could buy your way into heaven with money. The parable shows the joy one should experience in discovering the value of knowing Christ and serving Him.

I am compelled to preach. God had placed a great burden on Paul's heart to preach the gospel (Acts 9:1–16). This is similar to Jeremiah's burning heart to speak the truth of God (Jer. 20:9).

eager. Paul was ready to preach the gospel in Rome but had been prevented providentially so far. When God places a dream or longing on your heart, you must be sensitive to His timing and willing to be patient.

ambition. To "desire" earnestly. Paul was impassioned with taking the gospel to places where people had yet to hear the good news of Christ.

Paul is writing on the issue of how slaves should interact with their masters. Paul did not condone slavery, but his goal was not to restructure social institutions (1 Cor. 7:17–24). Paul wanted the Christian slaves to have a positive testimony through the way they worked. We can apply the principles here to how employees should work for their employers. These same principles should also be applied to how we serve in ministry.

9

notes:

Session

10

Finding My Ministry

Prepare for the Session

	READINGS	REFLECTIVE QUESTIONS
Monday	Romans 12:1	What will you do today to be more "holy and pleasing to God"?
Tuesday	Romans 12:2	How is your mind being transformed? What questions do you have about God's will for your life?
Wednesday	Romans 12:3	When have you thought of yourself "more highly than you ought"? What was the result?
Thursday	Romans 12:4–5	How comfortable are you with the truth that you belong to every other believer?
Friday	Romans 12:6–8	How are you doing at using your spiritual gifts?
Saturday	1 Corinthians 12:21–26	Do you treat those who seem "less honorable" with the same respect God does? Why or why not?
Sunday	Hebrews 13:15–16	Take some time to offer God a sacrifice of praise. Some ways to do this would be by thanking God for His sacrifice, telling others about that sacrifice, or doing acts of kindness.

notes:

BIBLE STUDY
- to understand that God wants everyone to have a ministry within His church
- to understand the value God places on every gift and each ministry
- to recognize how we need each other's ministry

LIFE CHANGE
- to commit our lives completely to Christ
- to stay away from distractions that may sidetrack us from serving Christ
- to be aware of our strengths and weaknesses
- to encourage the ministries of others
- to begin serving in a ministry within the body of Christ

Icebreaker (10-15 minutes)

Finding the Right Fit. Which one of the following statements most closely resembles your approach to shopping for clothes?

☐ I just buy it and take it home to try on. I can always return it if I don't like it.

☐ I bring someone with me to shop so I can try it on and get another opinion before making a decision about what to purchase.

☐ I bring my spouse or a friend along and let him or her pick out my clothes for me.

☐ I send my spouse shopping for me, and I wear whatever he or she brings home.

☐ I usually try on 10 different articles of clothing before deciding what I'm going to buy.

☐ I shop alone and make my own purchasing decisions about clothes.

☐ I order off the Internet or from a catalog.

10

notes:

LEARNING FROM THE BIBLE

ROMANS 12:1–8

Have a member of the class, selected ahead of time, read the passage in Romans.

Bible Study (30-45 minutes)

The Scripture for this week:

¹*Therefore, I urge you, brothers, in view of God's mercy, to offer your bodies as living sacrifices, holy and pleasing to God—this is your spiritual act of worship.* ²*Do not conform any longer to the pattern of this world, but be transformed by the renewing of your mind. Then you will be able to test and approve what God's will is— his good, pleasing and perfect will.*

³*For by the grace given me I say to every one of you: Do not think of yourself more highly than you ought, but rather think of yourself with sober judgment, in accordance with the measure of faith God has given you.* ⁴*Just as each of us has one body with many members, and these members do not all have the same function,* ⁵*so in Christ we who are many form one body, and each member belongs to all the others.* ⁶*We have different gifts, according to the grace given us. If a man's gift is prophesying, let him use it in proportion to his faith.* ⁷*If it is serving, let him serve; if it is teaching, let him teach;* ⁸*if it is encouraging, let him encourage; if it is contributing to the needs of others, let him give generously; if it is leadership, let him govern diligently; if it is showing mercy, let him do it cheerfully.*

notes:

...about today's session (5 minutes)

A PLACE TO BELONG

All around us people are looking for a place to belong. People want to be part of something significant—they want to feel needed. The search starts early in grade school as cliques develop. As kids grow older, much of the behavior exhibited in their middle and high school years is the result of a deep longing for acceptance and significance. However, growing into adulthood usually doesn't fulfill this need as <u>men and women enter unhealthy relationships out of a strong desire to be accepted and needed</u>. God knows that all of us have this deep desire for belonging and fellowship. Only through a personal relationship with Christ and fellowship with other believers will we find genuine significance and belonging. Happily, God has designed the church to be an environment of interdependence, where we give and receive encouragement, accountability, and giftedness.

Sadly, though, many believers go "to church" without being "part of the church." Why does this happen? <u>Because many have become satisfied with the routine and are more concerned about self than others</u>. The antidote to this disease of selfishness is to develop a deep love for God and others. In 1 Corinthians 13, Paul tells us that without love, all our religious activity is like a noisy cymbal. Serving one another and using our gifts comes out of a growing love for God and others. In today's session, we are going to learn how each of us can find our ministry and thus, fulfill the second greatest commandment to " 'love your neighbor as yourself' " (Mark 12:31).

notes:

10

109

Remain in groups of 6–8 people, in a horseshoe configuration.

In this small-group session, students will be responding to the following questions that will help them share their stories in terms of Paul's words to the Romans about becoming living sacrifices.

Have the students explore these questions together.

Identifying with the Story (5-7 minutes)

1. Which of the following activities would be most difficult to give up completely in your life?

   ☐ watching television
   ☐ listening to the radio
   ☐ reading the newspaper and magazines
   ☐ eating sweets and desserts
   ☐ using the cell phone
   ☐ going to the movies
   ☐ going shopping
   ☐ playing sports
   ☐ other:_____

2. Have you ever thought you were good at something and later discovered you weren't? What made you change your mind?

3. What actions or attitudes listed in this passage do you see in the members of your group?

notes:

Share with your class the following information which you may modify according to your own perspectives and teaching needs. The answers to the student book questions (provided in the margin) are underlined.

Complete this statement by circling the option that best fits: "If church were a football game, I would be ..."
• in the stands as a spectator;
• on the sidelines hoping to get in the game;
• on the field giving it everything I've got."

What are three basic truths we learn from Paul about finding our ministry?

What definition of ministry do we need to rediscover?

today's session (15-20 minutes)

The last 11 chapters of Romans provide us with some of the most treasured truths of God, including the way individuals come into a personal relationship with a Holy God. Paul writes about the "lostness" of mankind due to sin, the depravity of the human soul, the powerlessness of the Law to save, the necessity of grace and faith in justification, the sovereignty of God, and other magnificent doctrines. It is against this backdrop that Paul urges each believer to action. Unfortunately, many who claim to know Christ are too satisfied with knowing the facts of Christianity and going through the routine of church. They consider their "spiritual act of worship" their presence in an hour church service each week. Paul makes it very clear in our passage today that every believer has been given the responsibility to find his or her ministry and do it. As we look at our passage today and apply its truths to our lives, think about your own involvement in ministry and complete this sentence: "If church were a football game, I would be ... in the stands as a spectator; on the sidelines hoping to get in the game; on the field giving it everything I've got." Let's look at what Paul tells us about finding our ministry.

God Wants Everyone to Have a Ministry within His Church

Ministry is not just for the "super spiritual" or those who have graduated from seminary. God expects each believer to serve regardless of education or experience. God has called all Christians to be His ministers. Many people think that the only ministers in their church are those who are paid by the church. But ministry is not a privilege given to those who are in full-time vocational ministry. We need to rediscover what ministry really means. That definition of ministry is *to serve and meet the needs of others*. That's it. It's what all of us as believers are called to do. Churches who make little impact for the kingdom of God think that the work of God is done by "professional ministers." In Romans 12:3, Paul clarifies that he's writing to ALL Christians concerning their giftedness, not a particular group or the "spiritual elite": "*I say to every one of you:*" (italics added). God has given each person the ability to serve Him by serving other believers. In 1 Corinthians 12:7, Paul declares that the Holy Spirit has strengthened all believers with certain gifts so we might build up others: "Now to *each one* the manifestation of the Spirit is given for the common good" (italics added).

God Values Each Gift and Ministry

Because some gifts are more public than others, we often wrongly overrate the value of certain gifts. While we may not be gifted to preach like Billy Graham, our gifts are just as valuable to God. He will

10

today's session (cont'd)

hold us accountable only for the gifts He gives us. God values each gift, regardless of how insignificant we feel our particular gift is.

In the same way the different parts of your body contribute to the way it functions, each believer's ministry contributes to the way the body of Christ functions. In Romans 12:4, Paul reminds us: "Just as each of us has one body with many members, and these members do not all have the same function," God designed His body, the church, to function at its best when every person does his or her God-given part in ministry. In 1 Corinthians 12:21–25, Paul uses an analogy of the human body to explain how God values each person's giftedness:

What analogy does Paul use in 1 Corinthians 12:21–25 to explain how God values each person's giftedness?

> *The eye cannot say to the hand, "I don't need you!" And the head cannot say to the feet, "I don't need you!" On the contrary, those parts of the body that seem to be weaker are indispensable, and the parts that we think are less honorable we treat with special honor. And the parts that are unpresentable are treated with special modesty, while our presentable parts need no special treatment. But God has combined the members of the body and has given greater honor to the parts that lacked it, so that there should be no division in the body.*

Believers Need Each Other's Giftedness

Paul makes a striking statement in Romans 12:5: "Each member *belongs* to all the others" (italics added). This statement flies in the face of contemporary values that encourage independence and climbing our way to the top at the expense of others. As believers we are designed to give to and receive from one another. In Acts 4:32, we see this attitude at work in the early church: "All the believers were one in heart and mind. No one claimed that any of his possessions was his own, but they shared everything they had." In 1 Corinthians 12:25–26, Paul emphasizes our interdependence within the body of Christ: "Its parts should have equal concern for each other. If one part suffers, every part suffers with it; if one part is honored, every part rejoices with it." We need each other's gifts, ministry, and encouragement. When I don't use my gift, you get cheated. When you don't use your gift, I get cheated.

Unfortunately, some believers have developed an attitude similar to that of Moses when God first called him to deliver the Israelites out of Egyptian bondage. Moses gave excuse after excuse for why he wasn't the one to do the job. The first thing many believers think about when challenged to serve is their inability and why God can't use them.

When challenged to serve, what is the first thing many believers think about?

If Moses hadn't served, the Israelites would have been cheated! You may not be called to deliver a nation out of slavery, but a friend may need your help getting free from bondage to a particular sin. Your ministry could make the difference in his or her life. We serve because we need one another.

notes:

✋ Remain in groups of 6–8 people, in a horseshoe configuration.

In this small-group session, students will be applying the lessons of the text to their own lives through the following questions.

The students were asked (in the student book) to choose an answer for each question and explain why.

✝

Learning from the Story (5-7 minutes)

1. What are you currently doing to "renew your mind"? Is it working?

2. In your church, to what degree is there a sense that "each member belongs to all the others" (v. 5)? How well do the members of the body function together using their gifts?

3. How do you (or could you) use your gifts within the body of Christ? What keeps you from using your gifts more fully?

10

notes:

life change lessons (5-7 minutes)

Here are some steps to help you find your ministry.

Share with the class the following thoughts on how the lessons of this text might be applied today. The answers to the student book questions (provided in the margin) are underlined unless the question requires a personal answer.

What are five steps you can take to help you find your ministry?

1. <u>COMMIT YOUR LIFE COMPLETELY TO CHRIST</u>. Many Christians have become too easily satisfied with the crumbs the world offers, not realizing there's a grand banquet waiting for them if they'll just accept the invitation. You can find your greatest satisfaction and joy in life by serving Christ and trusting Him with your future. If Christ is not first in your life, then ministry for Him takes a back seat. A fulfilling ministry only comes out of the overflow of a personal relationship with Christ.

2. <u>STAY AWAY FROM DISTRACTIONS THAT MAY SIDE-TRACK YOU FROM SERVING CHRIST</u>. In Romans 12:2, Paul instructs believers, "Do not conform any longer to the pattern of this world." Because of your identity in Christ and the power of the Holy Spirit in you, you have the strength and discernment to withstand the lies the world throws at you concerning happiness, success, and behavior—but only if you stay focused on the joy of pursuing God and His purposes in this world.

3. <u>BE AWARE OF YOUR STRENGTHS AND WEAKNESSES</u>. In our previous studies, you have recorded some areas of strength where God has been equipping you for ministry. You need to be aware of the way God has been working in the areas of your personality, spiritual gifts, natural abilities, passions, and experiences. You need to be open to new ministries and opportunities to serve where God can use these strengths. In Romans 12:3, Paul reminds us to make a realistic assessment of our strengths, "Do not think of yourself more highly than you ought, but rather think of yourself with sober judgment." You need to know your strengths and to be honest about your weaknesses. Humility is not denying your strengths. It's being honest about your weaknesses.

How could you encourage the ministry of a fellow believer in the coming week?

4. <u>ENCOURAGE THE MINISTRIES OF OTHERS</u>. In the attempt to get plugged in, you can too easily fall into the comparison trap. The trap is usually set when you begin a particular ministry and then compare your efforts with others. The result is usually feelings of inferiority or inadequacy. When this happens, you can get discouraged or jealous. You must realize that God only wants you to become the best "you" He made you to be. He hasn't called you to be like anyone else. Paul stresses this in Romans 12:4–5: "Just as each of us has one body with many members, and these members do not all have the same function, so in Christ we who are many form one body, and each member belongs to all the others." When freed of the comparison trap, you can recognize

your uniqueness and value. Then you will be able to encourage and work alongside other gifted believers for one common goal of building the body of Christ for the glory of God.

5. <u>BEGIN SERVING IN A MINISTRY WITHIN THE BODY OF CHRIST</u>. Our gifts weren't given to us so we could hide them. In verses 6–8 of Romans 12, Paul stresses the importance of using the gifts we've been given. Notice the cadence in his writing as he writes to make this point: "If it is ... let him ... ." You will only be able to find the ministry that fits you best by serving wherever there's a need. Through the process of developing a servant heart and mind, you'll recognize the areas of ministry in which God wants you to invest. Even if you're not sure of your position on the team, don't stay on the sideline. Get in the game!

notes:

Caring Time (15-20 minutes)

Close by sharing prayer requests and praying for one another. During this time, pray for the ministries that each person in your subgroup is currently involved in or is praying about becoming a part of. In addition, pray for the concerns on the Prayer/Praise Report.

notes:

⊍ CARING TIME
Remain in groups of 6–8 people, in a horseshoe configuration.

Hand out the Prayer/ Praise Report to the entire group. Ask each subgroup to pray for the empty chair. Pray specifically for God to guide you to someone to bring next week to fill that chair.

After a sufficient time of prayer in subgroups, close in a corporate prayer. Say, "Next week we will talk about: 'Mentoring and Being Mentored.'"

Remind participants of the daily Scripture readings and reflective questions found on page 118.

10

BIBLE STUDY NOTES

✝

Reference Notes

Use these notes to gain further understanding
of the text as you study on your own.

ROMANS 12:1
ethics

Therefore. Christian ethics flow from Christian theology; Christian obedience is the response to Christian truth.

I urge you. With full apostolic authority, Paul exhorts Christians to live out what they believe.

in view of God's mercy. Paul has just declared God's amazing mercy (Rom. 11:30–32). A Christian's motivation to obedience is overwhelming gratitude for God's mercy.

bodies. The Christian lifestyle is not a matter of a mystical spirituality that transcends one's bodily nature. Rather, it is an everyday, practical exercise of love (Rom. 6:13; 13:8). The idea of "bodies" also emphasizes the metaphor of sacrifice since one puts bodies on the altar.

sacrifices. In the Old Testament sacrificial system, the sacrifice becomes wholly the property of God. It becomes holy, i.e., set apart for God only.

holy living

living ... holy ... pleasing to God. In Greek, these three phrases are attached with equal weight as qualifiers to "sacrifices." God sees our living sacrifices as a rejection of the world's values to live in accord with His principles (i.e., sanctification), and hence to be the kind of sacrifice God desires.

spiritual act of worship. Paul may mean by this an inner attitude on the part of a person toward God (in contrast to external rites). But since the word translated "spiritual" can be rendered "rational," the idea may be that believers render intelligent worship. This meaning is given credence by the emphasis in verse 2.

ROMANS 12:2
nonconformity

Do not conform. Literally, "stop allowing yourself to be conformed"; i.e., believers are no longer helpless victims of a sin-filled world system that would shape them into a distorted pattern; rather, they now have the ability and help to resist such influences.

be transformed. The force of the verb is "continue to let yourself be transformed"; i.e., a continuous action by the Holy Spirit which goes on for a lifetime. A Christian's responsibility is to stay open to this sanctification process as the Spirit works to teach him or her to look at life from God's reality.

renewing of your mind. Develop a spiritual sensitivity and perception—learn to see life from God's perspective. Paul emphasizes the need to develop an understanding of God's ways.

test and approve. Christians are called to a responsible freedom of choice and action, based on the inner, renewing work of the Holy Spirit.

ROMANS 12:3–8

Paul now turns to the Christian community as a whole—understanding it to be composed of believers with different gifts.

ROMANS 12:3
each believer

every one of you. The truth about spiritual gifts applies to each believer.

sober judgment. The command is to know oneself (especially one's gifts) accurately, rather than to have too high an opinion of oneself in comparison

✝

ROMANS 12:3
each believer
(cont'd)

to others. This attitude enables a body of believers to blend their gifts together in harmonious ministry.

measure of faith. Believers are not to measure themselves against others, but rather to evaluate themselves by how well they are living in accordance to what they know about how God wants His people to live.

ROMANS 12:4–5

Using a picture that could be understood in all cultures—the body—Paul defines the nature of the Christian community: diverse gifts, but all part of one body, the body of Christ.

ROMANS 12:5
interdependent

each member belongs to all the others. This is the critical insight that creates harmony in the church. Believers must recognize that they are interdependent, needing to give to and receive from one another.

ROMANS 12:6
gifts

gifts. Those endowments given by God to every believer by grace (the words *grace* and *gifts* come from the same root word) to be used in God's service. The gifts listed here (and elsewhere in the New Testament) are not meant to be exhaustive or absolute since no gift list overlaps completely.

prophesying. Inspired utterances, distinguished from teaching by their immediacy and unpremeditated nature, the source of which is direct revelation by God; often directed to concrete situations, at times about the future (Acts 11:27–28), at other times about what God will do (Acts 13:9–11); given by both men and women (Acts 21:9) and in words readily understood. Prophesying was highly valued in the New Testament church (1 Cor. 14:1).

in proportion to his faith. This could mean that prophets are to resist adding their own words to the prophecy, or it could mean that they must measure their utterances in accord with "the faith"; i.e. Christian doctrine.

ROMANS 12:7
service

serving. The special capacity for rendering practical service to the needy.

teaching. In contrast to the prophet (whose utterances are the direct revelation of God), the teacher relied on the Old Testament Scriptures and the teachings of Jesus to instruct others.

ROMANS 12:8
use your gift

Paul concludes his brief discussion of spiritual gifts with this emphasis on the fact that whatever gift one has, it should be exercised with enthusiasm for the good of others.

encouraging. This is supporting and assisting others to live a life of obedience to God.

contributing. The person who takes delight in giving away his or her possessions.

leadership. Those with special ability to guide a congregation are called upon to do so with zeal.

showing mercy. "The person whose special function is, on behalf of the congregation, to tend the sick, relieve the pain, or care for the aged or 'disabled.' "[1] Three of the seven gifts involve practical assistance to the needy.

[1] C.E.B. Cranfield, *The International Critical Commentary: A Critical and Exegetical Commentary on the Epistle to the Romans* (Edinburgh: T & T Clark, 1979), 627.

10

Session

11

Mentoring and Being Mentored

Prepare for the Session

	READINGS	REFLECTIVE QUESTIONS
Monday	Acts 16:1–2	What have you done in the past week that would cause other believers to speak well of you?
Tuesday	Acts 16:3	What sacrifices would you make to minister to those who need Christ?
Wednesday	Acts 16:4–5	How do you help strengthen others in the faith?
Thursday	2 Timothy 2:1–2	Who has mentored you and taught you about Christ? Show your appreciation to that person in some way this week.
Friday	Matthew 9:36–38	Pray for the "Lord of the harvest" to show you in what "field" He wants you to work.
Saturday	2 Timothy 4:5	Do you feel you are faithfully discharging the duties of your ministry? Why or why not?
Sunday	2 Timothy 3:10–14	How willing are you to let someone else know everything about you, as Paul did with Timothy? How would that help your ministry?

notes:

✝

OUR GOALS FOR THIS SESSION ARE:

🐴 **In groups of 6–8, gather people in a horseshoe configuration.**

Make sure everyone has a name tag.

Take time to share information on class parties that are coming up as well as any relevant church events.

INTRODUCE THE ICEBREAKER ACTIVITY: The students have been given instructions in their books.

After the Icebreaker say something like, "You probably don't want to go back to high school, but mentoring can be a crucial part of your success at work as an employee and in life as a Christian. This week we'll explore how to be a mentor and be mentored."

Hand out the Prayer/Praise Report. A sample copy is on pages 158–159. Have people write down prayer requests and praises. Then have the prayer coordinator collect the report and make copies for use during the Caring Time.

BIBLE STUDY
- to understand why we need to be mentored for ministry
- to understand the relational nature of mentoring
- to learn how Paul mentored Timothy in ministry

LIFE CHANGE
- to interview a successful mentor and learn from his or her experiences
- to place ourselves under a mentor who can help develop our ministry potential
- to reproduce ourselves in ministry by mentoring an emerging leader

Icebreaker   (10-15 minutes)

School Days. As you think back over your years in high school, in which of the following areas would you have benefited the most by having a personal mentor?

- ☐ studying a particular subject
- ☐ playing a sport
- ☐ learning to drive a car
- ☐ styling my hair
- ☐ relating to members of the opposite sex
- ☐ planning my career
- ☐ relating to my parents
- ☐ other:_____

notes:

11

**LEARNING FROM
THE BIBLE**

ACTS 16:1–5

**Select two members
of the class ahead of
time. Have one read
the passage from
Acts and the other
read the passage
from 2 Timothy.**

Bible Study   (30-45 minutes)

The Scripture for this week:

¹He came to Derbe and then to Lystra, where a disciple named Timothy lived, whose mother was a Jewess and a believer, but whose father was a Greek. ²The brothers at Lystra and Iconium spoke well of him. ³Paul wanted to take him along on the journey, so he circumcised him because of the Jews who lived in that area, for they all knew that his father was a Greek. ⁴As they traveled from town to town, they delivered the decisions reached by the apostles and elders in Jerusalem for the people to obey. ⁵So the churches were strengthened in the faith and grew daily in numbers.

¹You then, my son, be strong in the grace that is in Christ Jesus. ²And the things you have heard me say in the presence of many witnesses entrust to reliable men who will also be qualified to teach others.

2 TIMOTHY 2:1–2

notes:

**Summarize these
introductory remarks.
Be sure to include
the underlined
information, which
gives the answers
to the student book
questions (provided
in the margin).**

*How is church like
a football game?*

*What did the leader
say about the way
many churches
measure success?*

...about today's session (5 minutes)

REPRODUCTION

Church is much like a football game. There are two types of people at the game. There are 22 men on the field in desperate need of rest, but there are 50,000 people in the stands in desperate need of exercise! What can those of us who are in the game, serving in a ministry, do to get more people out of the stands and into the game? The answer is to mentor a potential leader. Reproduce yourself in ministry. This is God's plan for achieving His purposes. Jesus mentored His 12 disciples. Paul mentored Timothy. Elijah mentored Elisha. David mentored Solomon.

Today, many churches measure their success by their seating capacity. The focus of their ministry is on the "masses." The result is typically good, short-term growth that tends to fizzle out in the long run. In contrast, those churches that have experienced steady growth over many years have learned to value "sending capacity" rather than seating capacity. Sending capacity is the ability of a church to develop new leaders. It's been said, "Everything rises and

falls on leadership." But ministry development cannot remain the sole responsibility of the paid church staff if sustained growth is desired. <u>These few leaders don't have enough time or energy to provide all the leadership development needed. In healthy churches, persons who are not career ministers but who have leadership abilities are empowered to raise up and mentor new leaders</u>. So, where do we start? We start by asking another person to mentor us. Then, we look for someone else who wants to make a difference for God's kingdom and mentor him or her into a great leader. And we keep growing because we never reach a point where we no longer need mentoring. In today's session we're going to look at the mentoring relationship between Paul and Timothy and discover some valuable principles from their relationship.

Why can't we leave leadership development up to the paid church staff? What role should existing lay leaders play in mentoring new leaders?

notes:

☺ Remain in groups of 6–8 people, in a horseshoe configuration.

In this small-group session, students will be responding to the following questions that will help them share their stories in terms of Paul's mentoring of Timothy.

Have the students explore these questions together.

✝ Identifying with the Story (5-7 minutes)

1. In Acts 16:1–5, Paul asks Timothy to accompany him in ministering in several towns. Are you more like Paul, eager to mentor someone in ministry or are you more like Timothy, waiting for someone to mentor you?

2. If you could choose to go anywhere in the world on a mission trip, where would you go? Have you ever been on a mission trip outside the state in which you live? If so, where did you go?

3. Who has made the most significant impact in your spiritual development? How did this person help you mature in your faith?

   ☐ a parent   ☐ a minister
   ☐ my spouse   ☐ a close friend
   ☐ my children   ☐ a coworker
   ☐ a school teacher   ☐ other:_____
   ☐ a leader within my church

11

today's session (15-20 minutes)

Just one look at our society tells us that there is a seemingly insurmountable amount of work that needs to be done for God. In Matthew 9:36, we see Jesus taking a survey of the needs that surrounded Him in His day: "<u>When he saw the crowds, he had compassion on them, because they were harassed and helpless, like sheep without a shepherd</u>."

Mentoring Encourages and Equips

"Harassed and helpless" is an apt description of people in our society. We can look in our schools, government, families, our places of employment, or right next door and discover areas where the touch of Jesus is needed. But God doesn't expect us to carry it all on our shoulders. There's more work than any one person could ever think of doing. Jesus instructed His disciples in Matthew 9:37–38: " 'The harvest is plentiful but the workers are few. <u>Ask the Lord of the harvest, therefore, to send out workers into his harvest field</u>.' "

You can become an answer to this prayer. God is looking for people who will help develop new leaders who can start new small groups, serve in existing ministries, mentor others, and lead new ministries. If you are hesitant about mentoring others, here are some assumptions about people we can safely make which may help. <u>First, everyone wants to feel needed, to feel like they are making a difference with their lives</u>. Mentoring will help them feel worthwhile. <u>Second, everyone wants, needs, and desires to be encouraged. Third, leadership is best developed when there's a model to watch</u>. Mentoring allows people to see the principles and character of a leader modeled up close and personal. <u>Fourth, new leaders need to develop skills for ministry</u>. Mentoring transfers those skills more quickly than reading a book or listening to a tape. <u>Fifth, most people already have passions that are waiting to be developed into actions</u>.

In Acts 16:1–5, we see a snapshot of Paul's heart for mentoring as he takes Timothy along to assist him in ministry. Timothy needed the presence of a godly, spiritual man in his life who could be an example and model for him. Paul knew that Timothy would benefit from their mentoring relationship in several ways. We can reap those same benefits, and one of those benefits is gaining needed accountability. Each of us needs someone who will watch our lives and monitor our progress. We gain confidence for ministry when we know someone is walking right beside us, helping us "learn the ropes." A mentor helps us avoid the same mistakes that he or she made. Mentoring accelerates the leadership development process

Share with your class the following information which you may modify according to your own perspectives and teaching needs. The answers to the student book questions (provided in the margin) are underlined.

How did Jesus describe the crowds in Matthew 9:36? When you look around your community, what are the most obvious needs of the people?

In Matthew 9:37, what did Jesus tell his disciples to pray for? How can you be an answer to that prayer?

What are five safe assumptions we can make about people as we think about entering a mentoring relationship?

and puts us far ahead of where we would be if we tried to minister on our own. Eventually, those leaders that we've already mentored begin to mentor someone and God's work prospers.

Mentoring Requires a Personal Investment

We must also understand the nature of mentoring. It is a personal process, not a mechanical one. Mentoring does not necessarily rely on a program. It relies on a trusting relationship between two people—a leader and an emerging leader. We can readily see the personal nature of mentoring in Paul and Timothy's relationship. In 1 Timothy 1:2, Paul writes, "To Timothy my true son in the faith." We sense the emotion of young Timothy and the passion of Paul in 2 Timothy 1:4 as Paul wrote to Timothy, "Recalling your tears, I long to see you, so that I may be filled with joy." This was far from a mechanical, sterile relationship. Paul had a heart for Timothy and Timothy had a heart for Paul.

So let's say you have the desire to mentor an emerging leader for ministry. What will you need to invest in the person you're mentoring? In 2 Timothy 3:10–11, Paul describes some of the elements involved in mentoring Timothy. "You, however, know all about my teaching, my way of life, my purpose, faith, patience, love, endurance, persecutions, sufferings." Paul taught Timothy about faith in Christ ("my teaching"), gave him a lifestyle to emulate ("my way of life"), a purpose to pursue ("my purpose"), reasons to believe ("faith"), and showed him the strength and wisdom necessary to endure obstacles and difficulties along the way ("patience, love, endurance, persecutions, sufferings"). How did Timothy "know all about" Paul? Simply, Paul modeled it for him.

In 2 Timothy 3:10–11, Paul describes some of the elements involved in mentoring Timothy. List those here:

Mentoring Multiplies Leaders

After Paul mentored Timothy, he launched him into ministry on his own. Paul set him free, equipped to handle the responsibility of ministering and mentoring others for Christ. In 2 Timothy 2:1–2, Paul encourages Timothy with these words: "You then, my son, be strong in the grace that is in Christ Jesus. And the things you have heard me say in the presence of many witnesses entrust to reliable men who will also be qualified to teach others." That is the power of multiplication.

In 2 Timothy 3:14, we also see Paul's exhortation for Timothy to continue learning and using what he has learned: "As for you, continue in what you have learned and have become convinced of, because you know those from whom you learned it." Not only did Timothy gain practical insight for ministry, he also gained confidence because Paul modeled it for him. Timothy knew that the principles Paul instilled in his life were legitimate and tested.

11

today's session (cont'd)

What is the key to remember when mentoring?

Here's the key to remember when mentoring: <u>People do what people see</u>. What was the outcome of Paul's mentoring of Timothy?—"The churches were strengthened in the faith and grew daily in numbers" (Acts 16:5).

Jesus called two disciples with the words, " 'Come follow me ... and I will make you fishers of men' " (Matt. 4:19). The words of the Master-Mentor should be our invitation, too.

notes:

✚

Remain in groups of 6–8 people, in a horseshoe configuration.

In this small-group session, students will be applying the lessons of the text to their own lives through the following questions.

The students were asked (in the student book) to choose an answer for each question and explain why.

Learning from the Story (5-7 minutes)

1. Which of the following qualities is the most important to consider when selecting someone to mentor in ministry?

   ☐ teachable—"a disciple" (Acts 16:1)
   ☐ character—"spoke well of him" (Acts 16:2)
   ☐ listener—"the things you have heard me say" (2 Tim. 2:2)
   ☐ leadership potential—"entrust to reliable men who will also be qualified" (2 Tim. 2:2)

2. What do you think is the most common excuse for not mentoring someone for ministry?

   ☐ I'm not presently serving in a particular ministry.
   ☐ I just don't have the time.
   ☐ I don't believe I'm a very good example.
   ☐ I need to be mentored by someone else first.
   ☐ I'll leave mentoring up to our paid staff members.
   ☐ Other:_____

3. Who was most influential in leading you to Christ? Who led that person to Christ? And, who led that person to Christ? See how far back you can go. What does this tell us about the power of mentoring and discipling others?

life change lessons (5-7 minutes)

Share with the class the following thoughts on how the lessons of this text might be applied today. The answers to the student book questions (provided in the margin) are underlined unless the question requires a personal answer.

What are two steps you can take to help you get started in the mentoring process?

What this world needs are more leaders like Timothy. He was faithful, available, and teachable. But in spite of his willingness, he still needed a mature Christian mentor to bring his leadership abilities to the front. Timothy became a great force for the kingdom through Paul's mentoring. We must take the initiative like Paul and bring other emerging leaders under our wings and help them become all that God has called them to be. Often, the most difficult part of doing something we know we should do is just getting started. Here are some steps you can take to help you get started in the mentoring process:

1. <u>INTERVIEW A SUCCESSFUL MENTOR AND LEARN FROM HIS OR HER EXPERIENCES</u>. Once you begin developing ministry skills, you need to be a good steward of them. A good place to start is to talk with a successful mentor who can give you insight into how to reproduce yourself in ministry. Timothy was able to carry out the instruction of Paul in 2 Timothy 2:2 because he had learned from a successful mentor (Paul).

2. <u>PLACE YOURSELF UNDER A MENTOR WHO CAN HELP DEVELOP YOUR MINISTRY POTENTIAL</u>. No one ever gets to a place where he or she no longer needs to learn from others. Once you think you know everything you need to know about life and ministry, you are thrown a curve. Only so much can be learned from books and conferences. You need to be mentored by someone who has the character, perseverance, wisdom, and ministry skills that you want to emulate. "Plans fail for lack of counsel, but with many advisers they succeed" (Prov. 15:22).

REPRODUCE YOURSELF IN MINISTRY BY MENTORING AN EMERGING LEADER. Here are some tips for mentoring an emerging leader:

What are six tips you can use for mentoring an emerging leader?

Look for Emerging Leaders: Emerging leaders have strong people skills, a positive attitude, self-discipline, and proven character.

Lead by Example: Your ability to teach never exceeds your success in modeling what you are teaching.

Listen to Their Hearts: You must learn what motivates them and understand their goals and dreams. Learn their strengths and weaknesses.

Labor Alongside Them: This allows them to ask questions and try out ministry with a "safety net." They may not have enough nerve to try a ministry on their own. Your assistance will provide the encouragement they need.

11

125

life change lessons (cont'd)

Look for Teachable Moments: It really is true that we learn best by experience. Look for those moments when you will be able to highlight a particular principle or bit of wisdom.

Launch Them Into Ministry: Just as a mother bird pushes her growing chicks out of the nest, we must allow developing leaders to get out of our boat and into one of their own. You can be the person that launches them to go places they never thought they could! As a result, your ministry will be multiplied.

notes:

⏻ CARING TIME
Remain in groups of 6–8 people, in a horseshoe configuration.

Hand out the Prayer/ Praise Report to the entire group. Ask each subgroup to pray for the empty chair. Pray specifically for God to guide you to someone to bring next week to fill that chair.

After a sufficient time of prayer in subgroups, close in a corporate prayer. Say, "Next week we will talk about: 'Working on a Team.'"

Remind participants of the daily Scripture readings and reflective questions found on page 128.

Caring Time (15-20 minutes)

Close by sharing prayer requests and praying for one another. During this time, pray that God would provide each group member with a wise and caring mentor, and with an emerging leader to mentor in ministry. In addition, pray for the concerns on the Prayer/Praise Report.

notes:

✝

Reference Notes

Use these notes to gain further understanding
of the text as you study on your own.

ACTS 16:1–3
honoring tradition

As the son of a Jewish woman, Jewish law said Timothy ought to have been circumcised as an infant. Perhaps his Gentile father (who apparently was dead at the time of Paul's visit) had forbidden it. Since there is no mention of a synagogue in Lystra, his mother may not have been able to practice the Jewish traditions very seriously. (Her marriage to a Gentile was also a violation of Jewish law.) At any rate, for Timothy, a Jew, to accompany Paul required adherence to the Jewish custom of circumcision. Anything else would communicate to other Jews that he had no regard whatsoever for their honored traditions. To avoid that offense, Timothy was circumcised. This is a further illustration of his (and Timothy's) willingness to accommodate himself to cultural sensitivities.

ACTS 16:4
salvation

decisions reached by the apostles and elders in Jerusalem. These decisions regarded the question of how Gentiles were saved and whether they needed to obey the Law of Moses in order to gain salvation (see Acts 15:10–11,23–29).

ACTS 16:5
strong faith

strengthened. Refers to churches "being made solid or firm" in the faith taught by Christ and the apostles.

1 TIMOTHY 2:1
grace

grace. Grace is the sphere within which the Christian lives and moves. *in Christ Jesus.* The source of grace is union with Christ through saving faith.

1 TIMOTHY 2:2
entrusted

Just as the gospel has been entrusted to Timothy (1 Tim. 6:20; 2 Tim. 1:14) so he is to entrust it to others who, in turn, teach it to yet others. This whole process of "entrusting" is made doubly important by the fact that Paul will soon call Timothy to join him in Rome (which means that others will have to take over the teaching ministry in Ephesus).

notes:

11

Session

12

Working on a Team

Prepare for the Session

	READINGS	REFLECTIVE QUESTIONS
Monday	Nehemiah 2:17–18	How do you need the gracious hand of God to help you this week?
Tuesday	Nehemiah 2:19	Have you ever been falsely accused? How did you respond?
Wednesday	Nehemiah 2:20	For what situation in your life do you need the assurance that the God of heaven will give you success?
Thursday	Nehemiah 4:6	What ministry are you working at with all your heart?
Friday	Nehemiah 8:1–3,5–6	What could you do to make your worship more meaningful?
Saturday	Nehemiah 9:5–6	How does this prayer of praise help you understand God's character? Write your own prayer of praise to God.
Sunday	Nehemiah 12:43	Can others see the joy in you that comes from knowing God? How can you spread that joy today?

notes:

✝

OUR GOALS FOR THIS SESSION ARE:

⊙ In groups of 6–8, gather people in a horseshoe configuration.

Make sure everyone has a name tag.

Take time to share information on class parties that are coming up as well as any relevant church events.

INTRODUCE THE ICEBREAKER ACTIVITY: The students have been given instructions in their books.

After the Icebreaker say something like, "Nehemiah faced a daunting challenge—rebuilding the wall around an entire city. To do that quickly, he needed committed teamwork from everyone. This week's session will look at God's team, where no one position is more important than any other."

Hand out the Prayer/Praise Report. A sample copy is on pages 158-159. Have people write down prayer requests and praises. Then have the prayer coordinator collect the report and make copies for use during the Caring Time.

BIBLE STUDY
- to understand why we need to serve on a ministry team
- to recognize the importance of leadership on a ministry team
- to understand the power of a vision for a ministry team

LIFE CHANGE
- to clearly define the purpose of the team
- to eliminate distractions to the work of the team
- to work with the attitude of a servant
- to communicate openly with other team members

 Icebreaker (10-15 minutes)

Positions, Everyone! If your church was challenged by another church to play a game of football, which position on the team would you most likely volunteer to play and why?

☐ quarterback   ☐ wide receiver
☐ lineman (blocker) ☐ kicker
☐ coach   ☐ cheerleader
☐ statistician   ☐ water boy
☐ team mascot   ☐ other:_____
☐ play-by-play announcer

notes:

12

LEARNING FROM THE BIBLE

NEHEMIAH 2:17–20

Have a member of the class, selected ahead of time, read the passage from Nehemiah.

Bible Study   (30-45 minutes)

The Scripture for this week:

¹⁷Then I said to them, "You see the trouble we are in: Jerusalem lies in ruins, and its gates have been burned with fire. Come, let us rebuild the wall of Jerusalem, and we will no longer be in disgrace." ¹⁸I also told them about the gracious hand of my God upon me and what the king had said to me. They replied, "Let us start rebuilding." So they began this good work.

¹⁹But when Sanballat the Horonite, Tobiah the Ammonite official and Geshem the Arab heard about it, they mocked and ridiculed us. "What is this you are doing?" they asked. "Are you rebelling against the king?"

²⁰I answered them by saying, "The God of heaven will give us success. We his servants will start rebuilding, but as for you, you have no share in Jerusalem or any claim or historic right to it."

notes:

...about today's session (5 minutes)

ALL FOR ONE

Summarize these introductory remarks. Be sure to include the underlined information, which gives the answers to the student book questions (provided in the margin).

What are some examples that show we're living primarily in a "what's-in-it-for-me" generation?

Have you noticed <u>even professional sports teams that once epitomized the essence and value of teamwork are becoming more known for the individual rewards, contract disputes, and individual "stars" drawing attention to themselves</u>? We seem to be living primarily in a "what's-in-it-for-me" generation. A movie entitled, *Remember the Titans*, which was based on a true story, instead reminds us of the power of teamwork in accomplishing something great.

In 1971, the city of Alexandria, Virginia was ordered by the courts to integrate its schools. This meant that their two high school football teams would also have to integrate. As a result, a coaching change was ordered. Bill Yoast, the popular head coach of T.C. Williams High School, was replaced by a newcomer, Herman Boone. The problem with this coaching change was based on the fact that Boone was black and Yoast was white. Boone was up against difficult circumstances as the majority of the town expressed its outrage. In fact, if he lost a game, he would have lost his job. So, what did Boone do to keep his job? He focused on two things. First, he had to bring together two teams and make them into one. The pivotal scene in the movie was Boone convincing Yoast to remain as his assistant coach. The cooperation between these two leaders became an example for the way the black and white players could overcome their differences and play together. However, convincing the players to look beyond race and learn to respect each other as fellow teammates was just the beginning. Boone had to develop in his players a deep sense of personal discipline. They needed to learn the value of hard work and giving up personal glory for the well-being of the team. Boone's work paid off as the T. C. Williams' Titans went on to win the Virginia State championship.

What lesson can we learn about teamwork from the true story involving two football teams that came together to win the Virginia State High School championship in 1971?

<u>*Remember the Titans* shows us that individual glory and gratification should be a low priority compared to doing your best for the sake of the team</u>. A classic summary of this truth is the pledge of The Three Musketeers, "All for one, and one for all." Today, we're going to look at how to be a team player within a community of believers. We'll do this by looking at the example given us by Nehemiah.

notes:

12

⊕

○ Remain in groups of 6–8 people, in a horseshoe configuration.

In this small-group session, students will be responding to the following questions that will help them share their stories in terms of the story about Nehemiah and the rebuilding of the wall around Jerusalem.

Have the students explore these questions together.

Identifying with the Story (5-7 minutes)

1. In chapter 2, Nehemiah asked King Artaxerxes for permission to rebuild the wall around Jerusalem. He asked for time off to travel to a distant country. He asked for supplies and materials. He asked for references so he could pass through certain areas. He asked for assistance with the accompaniment of the king's army. Which of the following would you find most difficult to ask your boss (or previous boss if not presently working)?

   ☐ a salary increase
   ☐ increased vacation time
   ☐ more resources to do my job
   ☐ a job reference for an interview with another employer (assuming you have already put in two-weeks notice)
   ☐ a personal/administrative assistant to help with my tasks

2. In chapter 3, we read of the teamwork that Nehemiah had inspired in Nehemiah 2:17–20. What was the best team experience you've been a part of—sports-related or otherwise? What made it such a fulfilling experience?

3. If you were in Nehemiah's position, how would you have most likely responded to the mocking and ridiculing of Sanballat, Tobiah, and Geshem?

   ☐ I would have formed a committee to look into the situation.
   ☐ I would have gone back home.
   ☐ I would have taken a vote from the people to see if they still wanted to rebuild the wall.
   ☐ I would have questioned whether I really heard from God.
   ☐ I would have told them to mind their own business.
   ☐ I would have asked them, "If God is for us then who can be against us?"
   ☐ Other:_____

notes:

Share with your class the following information which you may modify according to your own perspectives and teaching needs. The answers to the student book questions (provided in the margin) are underlined.

today's session (15-20 minutes)

As we look at the example of Nehemiah, we'll examine it to gain insight into how he generated a spirit of teamwork and cooperation to do God's work. Simply putting people into a group and giving them an assignment won't develop a team. Successful teams are built intentionally. What do we need to know about how to develop and work together on a team? Here are several insights from Nehemiah's experience that will help us understand the importance of using our gifts in the context of a "team" of believers.

We Need to Understand Why We Need to Serve on a Ministry Team

Nehemiah knew he couldn't rebuild the wall around Jerusalem alone. He needed help. The importance of his assembled team of workers was so important to this ministry project that in chapter 3, Nehemiah listed those involved and the details of their work. Nehemiah understood the principle found in Ecclesiastes 4:9–12, that they could accomplish far more as a team than any one person could do alone. That is the power of Christian community. We don't serve in isolation. Rather, we serve with others who are committed to the same work we are doing. Our ministry is maximized when we join hands with other committed workers. Here are several benefits that come through partnering with others on a team.

What are four benefits that come through partnering with others on a team?

First, a team of individuals brings several perspectives into the group, allowing for better decisions and an increased capacity for seeing new opportunities. Second, serving on a team provides encouragement and accountability for following through on commitments. Third, working on a team brings out the best of our gifts and abilities. Our gifts are designed to complement one another because our abilities and gifts are magnified when we are surrounded by other committed team members. As someone once said, "None of us is as smart as all of us." Fourth, we gain the strength to accomplish our dreams for ministry as we tap into the resources of the team members collectively. Keep in mind, "Few people are successful unless a lot of other people want them to be."[1]

We Need to See the Importance of Leadership in a Ministry Team

The fact is, all of us who exert influence on others are leaders. If we have no one following us, we are only taking a walk. Nehemiah's leadership set the tone for the team of workers who set out to rebuild the wall. If you haven't learned this truth by now, there's no time like the present: Everything rises and falls on leadership!

12

today's session (cont'd)

What did the leader mean by, "Everything rises and falls on leadership"?

Great leaders possess the knowledge of how to motivate and persuade people. Nehemiah knew that the people of Israel had great pride in their past and would be eager to regain their standing as a people. In verse 17, Nehemiah encourages them to, "Come, let us rebuild the wall of Jerusalem, and we will no longer be in disgrace."

We see from Nehemiah's experience that leaders set the tone and create the environment for the work that is to be done. This is true of the senior minister of a church as well as leaders of small-group Bible studies. It's been said that if you want to measure the temperature of a group, just stick a thermometer in the leader's mouth.

As you serve on a ministry team, never underestimate the power of leadership. People won't buy into a vision unless they buy into the leader first. You are a leader if you have influence. All of us are leaders to some degree if we are using our gifts faithfully in ministry. Is God calling you to be a Nehemiah? To rebuild a "wall" that has been broken down in your life? Leaders don't wait for someone else to act. They become burdened about something that matters to God and then act while trusting God for His timing and provision.

We Need to See the Power of a Vision for a Ministry Team

Define vision as the leader described it.

Vision can be defined as a mental picture of a preferred future. As we work on a team, we need a vision to propel us and motivate us. Baseball teams have a mental picture of what it is like to win a World Series. Football teams have a mental picture of what it is like to win a Super Bowl. A vision is the snapshot of that which "could" be and that which "should" be, as opposed to what actually is.

Why is it important for a team to have a vision?

If you think about it, all of us have a vision for our marriages, for our children, for our careers, for the rest of our lives. We may not have written it down or told anyone, but we do have a vision. Visions motivate us and give us a road map. Decisions for your ministry team become easier with a stated vision. If a choice will draw you away from the vision, then the answer is "no." If a choice will draw you closer to the vision, then the answer is "yes." Vision helps us prioritize our values.

How does having a vision keep us from getting distracted?

Nehemiah had a vision for seeing the wall rebuilt around Jerusalem. How do we know that he had a vision? In verse 20, in answering the mocking and ridicule, he declared, "The God of heaven will give us success." He already saw the walls rebuilt in his mind. He knew what success looked like! His vision was God-given, straight from heaven. That vision drove him. He would not allow himself to be distracted by criticism from outsiders or turmoil from insiders. His vision kept him focused on his ministry.

What is your vision for ministry? What do you see God doing with your gifts, abilities, experiences, personality, and passions? If you don't have a burden, ask God to show you broken-down "walls" that you can help rebuild. One of the most gratifying experiences in life is developing a God-given vision for ministry and joining with other believers to see it fulfilled. This is what Peter and Jesus' other disciples experienced in the early church. Their vision for taking the gospel to the Jews and Gentiles brought them together as a team of believers who were willing to die for their faith.

What are you willing to sacrifice to be on God's team and meet the needs of His people and His work?

notes

12

Remain in groups of 6–8 people, in a horseshoe configuration.

In this small-group session, students will be applying the lessons of the text to their own lives through the following questions.

The students were asked (in the student book) to choose an answer for each question and explain why.

Learning from the Story (5-7 minutes)

1. In what area of your community do you have the greatest burden for "broken-down walls"?

   ☐ schools   ☐ poor and needy
   ☐ pollution   ☐ crime and violence
   ☐ churches   ☐ government
   ☐ marriage   ☐ other:_____
   ☐ immoral lifestyles

2. What was the most recent step of faith you took where you knew the hand of God was upon you? How did you know? What was the result?

3. Think back to the last time you were ridiculed or criticized for doing something God told you to do. How did you feel? How did you respond? Looking back on the experience, is there anything you would change about the way you handled it?

notes:

life change lessons (5-7 minutes)

Share with the class the following thoughts on how the lessons of this text might be applied today. The answers to the student book questions (provided in the margin) are underlined unless the question requires a personal answer.

What are four keys to help you contribute the most to a team?

What does a "win" look like in your church? In your ministry?

A commonly used acronym for TEAM is Together Each Accomplishes More. While each of us may be individually equipped for ministry, God intends for us to minister alongside one another. Tremendous energy and creativity emerge when a team of individuals who are committed to the same vision for ministry come together to think, plan, and work. Here are four keys to help you contribute the most to a team:

1. CLEARLY DEFINE THE PURPOSE OF THE TEAM. In verse 17, Nehemiah clearly defines what he came to the city to do: "You see the trouble we are in: Jerusalem lies in ruins, and its gates have been burned with fire. Come, let us rebuild the wall of Jerusalem, and we will no longer be in disgrace." In Nehemiah's day, a city that was not protected by a wall was considered a disgrace because it was defenseless against attack and invasion. Nehemiah wanted to restore Jerusalem's ability to bring glory to God. He knew that the people needed a common goal. He knew they needed a rallying point. Teams are not very motivated when they are never sure if they have won! Teams need to know what a win looks like. Does everyone in your church understand what the purpose of the church is and what a "win" looks like? If no one has a good grasp on the purpose, then the members will not be very motivated. The same holds true for ministry teams. When using your gifts in an established ministry, make sure that the purpose of the team is clear and well-defined. Everyone must be on the same page.

Is there anything in your life right now that is distracting you from serving in ministry? What will help you stay focused on what God is calling you to do?

2. ELIMINATE DISTRACTIONS TO THE WORK OF THE TEAM. Many people launch great endeavors with a fast start only to be diverted by distractions. Nehemiah, though, incurred some potential distractions right from the outset. In verse 18, we see Nehemiah and the people beginning the work of rebuilding the wall. In verse 19, we read of criticism and ridicule directed at Nehemiah by Sanballat the Horonite, Tobiah the Ammonite official, and Geshem the Arab. They asked, "Are you rebelling against the king?" Nehemiah dealt with this potential distraction by confronting his detractors quickly and directly. We see later, as events unfold, that Nehemiah continues to face potential distractions to the work God had called him to. Nehemiah's response in 6:3 is a great picture of his ability to focus on what's important, eliminating distractions in order to do the work that God had given him: " 'I am carrying on a great project and cannot go down.' " As we serve in ministry, we can become easily distracted if we focus on the minors instead of the majors. Solve problems quickly and keep to the task at hand.

12

life change lessons (cont'd)

3. <u>WORK WITH A SERVANT'S HEART</u>. Nehemiah knew the work of his assembled team would be accomplished with individuals who didn't clamor for power or fame. They remembered who they were serving. In verse 20, he says, "We his servants will start rebuilding." As Jesus developed a team of disciples in his earthly ministry, He instilled the value of servanthood in their lives. He even modeled it by washing their feet. Teams work best when it doesn't matter who gets the credit. Usually, our natural tendency is to take the credit rather than share the blame. A servant is eager to share the blame and give the credit.

4. <u>COMMUNICATE OPENLY WITH OTHER TEAM MEMBERS</u>. Poor communication is probably the number 1 barrier to teams working effectively. Communication must be quick and accurate. In verse 18, Nehemiah takes time to tell the people all the things God had done to lead him to rebuild the wall. As we minister with others, we must be willing to explain the vision, be good listeners, and let team members use their gifts.

Caring Time   (15-20 minutes)

Close by sharing prayer requests and praying for one another. During this time, pray that God would give each person the heart of a servant as he or she works with a team of believers. In addition, pray for the concerns on the Prayer/Praise Report.

CARING TIME
Remain in groups of 6–8 people, in a horseshoe configuration.

Hand out the Prayer/ Praise Report to the entire group. Ask each subgroup to pray for the empty chair. Pray specifically for God to guide you to someone to bring next week to fill that chair.

After a sufficient time of prayer in subgroups, close in a corporate prayer. Say, "Next week we will talk about: How Do I Fit Into God's Plan?'"

Remind participants of the daily Scripture readings and reflective questions found on page 140.

notes:

✝

Reference Notes

Use these notes to gain further understanding
of the text as you study on your own.

BIBLE STUDY NOTES

NEHEMIAH 2:17
ruins

ruins. The walls and gates of the city around Jerusalem were left in ruins by Nebuchadnezzar in 586 B.C. as the Babylonians took the city captive and destroyed Solomon's temple. Eventually, the Babylonians were conquered by the Persian king, Cyrus. Cyrus gave the Jews permission to return to Jerusalem to rebuild the temple. This was accomplished under the leadership of Zerubbabel. However, the walls remained in ruins until Nehemiah showed up.

NEHEMIAH 2:18
God's timing

my God ... and ... the king. Nehemiah was cupbearer to Artaxerxes, the king of Persia. God gave Nehemiah a great burden to rebuild the walls around his ancestors' great city. But he couldn't just resign and go. Through providential timing and circumstances, the king gave Nehemiah permission and the supplies needed to rebuild the wall around Jerusalem. Nehemiah wanted the people to know that God was the cornerstone of this project and that the king had given his approval. Nehemiah knew that he needed to assure the people that this was a task worthy of their efforts.

NEHEMIAH 2:19
enemies

Sanballat. He was the chief political opponent of Nehemiah and was governor over Samaria.

Tobiah. He was likely the governor of Transjordan under the Persians. The opposition from these two individuals was probably political in nature because they felt their authority was threatened by Nehemiah.

Geshem. He was most likely in charge of a north Arabian confederacy involving a lucrative spice trade. He may have felt Nehemiah's presence would restrict trade and interfere with his profit-making abilities.

Are you rebelling against the king? This was an attempt to intimidate Nehemiah and his workers as well as induce the king of Persia to rethink his permission for Nehemiah to rebuild the walls. It may have been early "spin doctoring" to plant doubt and fear of participating in the people. Treason was punishable by death.

NEHEMIAH 2:20
no claim

you have no share ... claim ... historic right. These three opponents were not citizens of Jerusalem and did not belong to the tribes of Israel. Zerubbabel gave a similar answer to the Samaritans in Ezra 4:3. Because they were not Jews, they had no part in Nehemiah's vision.

notes:

12

¹Quote by Charles Brower, *Leadership Wired*, March, 1999, 2:8, www.injoy.com.

Session

13

How Do I Fit Into God's Plan?

Prepare for the Session

	READINGS	REFLECTIVE QUESTIONS
Monday	Jeremiah 29:10–12	Do you believe that God plans every event in your life to prosper you—not harm you? Why or why not?
Tuesday	Jeremiah 29:13–14	Have you sought God with all your heart?
Wednesday	Matthew 6:33	What does it mean to you to seek first the kingdom of God?
Thursday	Romans 8:28–29	How Christlike are you in your words, thoughts, and actions?
Friday	1 Thessalonians 4:3,7	How do you need God's help in living a holier life?
Saturday	1 Thessalonians 5:16–18	How often do you thank God for your circumstances and seek His will? Take some time in prayer to do just that.
Sunday	Proverbs 3:5–6	In what "ways" or areas of your life do you need to acknowledge the Lord and trust him with all your heart?

notes:

OUR GOALS FOR THIS SESSION ARE:

⊌ **In groups of 6–8, gather people in a horseshoe configuration.**

Make sure everyone has a name tag.

Take time to share information on class parties that are coming up as well as any relevant church events.

INTRODUCE THE ICEBREAKER ACTIVITY: The students have been given instructions in their books.

After the Icebreaker say something like, "Your favorite activities probably brought you great happiness. Today's session will help you see the joy in serving God."

Hand out the Prayer/Praise Report. A sample copy is on pages 158-159. Have people write down prayer requests and praises. Then have the prayer coordinator collect the report and make copies for use during the Caring Time.

BIBLE STUDY	• to understand that the core of God's plan is to bring persons into an eternal relationship with Himself
	• to understand God's primary desire is to make us like Christ
	• to realize that God's plan determines how He's shaped us for ministry
LIFE CHANGE	• to know God more intimately by scheduling a daily devotional time
	• to listen to God's voice by reading the Bible daily
	• to trust God's timing more than our own

Icebreaker   (10-15 minutes)

Joining the Cabinet. If a newly elected president of the United States renamed all of the cabinet positions similar to the following, which one would you most likely be appointed to?

- ☐ Secretary of Spunk (Energy)
- ☐ Secretary of Money (Treasury)
- ☐ Secretary of Fighting Battles (Defense)
- ☐ The Law of the Land (Attorney General)
- ☐ Secretary of Gardening (Agriculture)
- ☐ Secretary of Shopping (Commerce)
- ☐ Secretary of Hard Work (Labor)
- ☐ Secretary of Health and Well-Being (Health and Human Services)
- ☐ Secretary of Interior Decorating (Interior)
- ☐ Secretary of Travel (Transportation)
- ☐ Secretary of Boxing Up and Moving (Housing and Urban Development)
- ☐ Secretary of Reading (Education)
- ☐ Secretary of Honor (Veteran Affairs)

notes:

13

LEARNING FROM
THE BIBLE

**LEARNING FROM
THE BIBLE**

JEREMIAH 29:10–14

**Have a member of
the class, selected
ahead of time,
read the passage
from Jeremiah.**

Bible Study (30-45 minutes)

The Scripture for this week:

¹⁰*This is what the Lord says: "When seventy years are completed for Babylon, I will come to you and fulfill my gracious promise to bring you back to this place.* ¹¹*For I know the plans I have for you," declares the Lord, "plans to prosper you and not to harm you, plans to give you hope and a future.* ¹²*Then you will call upon me and come and pray to me, and I will listen to you.* ¹³*You will seek me and find me when you seek me with all your heart.* ¹⁴*I will be found by you," declares the Lord, "and will bring you back from captivity. I will gather you from all the nations and places where I have banished you," declares the Lord, "and will bring you back to the place from which I carried you into exile."*

notes:

**Summarize these
introductory remarks.
Be sure to include
the underlined
information, which
gives the answers
to the student book
questions (provided
in the margin).**

*Why is it easier to
put together a jigsaw
puzzle when you
have the puzzle
box cover?*

*Why do so many
Christians experience
frustration when
trying to figure
out how to fit
into God's plan?*

...about today's session (5 minutes)

YOU'RE PART OF GOD'S PLAN

Have you ever put together a large jigsaw puzzle? Have you ever put one together without the box cover? Those are two totally different experiences. <u>Trying to fit the pieces together without knowing what the big picture looks like is very frustrating.</u> You might just give up after a while. <u>The process is much easier when you have the picture that shows how everything fits together</u>.

<u>Many Christians get frustrated in their search for how their piece of life and ministry fits into God's larger plan because only God can see the box cover.</u> How can we make the process easier? We need to take a look at what the Bible tells us about what God's big picture looks like. Today, we're pulling out the puzzle box so we can more easily see how we fit into God's plan. We're going to start by looking in Jeremiah at God's great plan for His people, Israel, who had been in exile for 70 years.

⛉ **Remain in groups of 6–8 people, in a horseshoe configuration.**

In this small-group session, students will be responding to the following questions that will help them share their stories in terms of God's plan for His people, Israel.

Have the students explore these questions together.

Identifying with the Story (5-7 minutes)

1. Israel was in exile for 70 years before God allowed them to return. Which of the following times in your life seemed like the most difficult wait?

   ☐ between getting my learner's permit and my driver's license
   ☐ between a job interview and the job offer
   ☐ between my engagement and wedding day
   ☐ between the beginning of my senior year in high school and graduation
   ☐ between Christmas Eve and Christmas morning as a child
   ☐ other:_____

2. In our passage today, we learn that God had great plans for his people, Israel. Which of the following bring out your best planning skills?

   ☐ a vacation
   ☐ a date or night out on the town
   ☐ a party
   ☐ a wedding
   ☐ a home improvement project
   ☐ other:_____

3. God told His people that if they sought Him with all their hearts they would find Him. Which of the following things took the most effort for you to find?

   ☐ my spouse
   ☐ my job
   ☐ my house
   ☐ my car
   ☐ my church
   ☐ familiarity with a new city
   ☐ a gift for someone I care about
   ☐ other:_____

notes:

13

Share with your class the following information which you may modify according to your own perspectives and teaching needs. The answers to the student book questions (provided in the margin) are underlined.

today's session (15-20 minutes)

Although our passage in Jeremiah 29 is directed specifically at God's people, Israel, the truth of the verse applies to all of His children—then and now: God has a great plan for our lives. And probably every believer, at one time or another, has wondered what that particular plan is. Unfortunately, many Christians get frustrated trying to "decode" God's plan. The Bible, however, has already revealed God's overall purpose and plan. What do we need to know about God's plan and how we can fit into it? Let's look at three different aspects of God's plan.

The Core of God's Plan Is Adding Souls to His Kingdom

As we seek to discover how we fit into God's plan, we first need to understand what God's overarching plan for mankind is. In Luke 8:1 we read, "After this, Jesus traveled about from one town and village to another, proclaiming the good news of the kingdom of God." In Luke 19:10 we read, " 'For the Son of Man came to seek and to save what was lost.' "

In Ephesians 1:9–10, Paul tells us that God's plan is to build a kingdom where Christ is the ruler: "He made known to us the mystery of his will according to his good pleasure, which he purposed in Christ, to be put into effect when the times will have reached their fulfillment—to bring all things in heaven and on earth together under one head, even Christ." Where do we as believers fit into this plan? God is calling people into relationship with His Son, Jesus Christ, for their joy and His glory. In Matthew 6:33, Jesus instructs us "Seek first his kingdom and his righteousness."

What did the leader say is God's providential will?

As we think about God's plan, some theologians describe those things that God is going to do no matter what as His providential will. In Job 23:13 we see His resolve: "He stands alone, and who can oppose him? He does whatever he pleases." Some examples of God's providential will include Jesus' death on the cross for us and His return one day to gather His children. There are things that God has providentially decided to do without our input. Building His kingdom is part of His providential will. All of us can participate in His plan to bring people into His kingdom by spreading the good news of Christ. In fact, as Matthew 6:33 tells us, His kingdom should be first on our list of priorities.

How does God want all believers to participate in building His kingdom?

God's Primary Desire for My Life Is to Make Me Christlike

Not only does God want us to participate in building a spiritual kingdom for His glory by beginning a friendship with Him, but He also wants each of us to grow in "Christlikeness." In Romans 8:29, Paul shows us what God's plan has been all along: "For those God foreknew he also predestined to be conformed to the likeness of his Son." We can know that we are fitting into God's plan by growing in Christ. God's will is more about who I am than where I go or what I do. The challenge is: How do I become more Christlike?

How can you be in the "right place" and still not be a part of God's plan?

Why is this true? Because, if you're the "wrong person" (walking in sin) in the "right place" (i.e., right job or ministry), you still won't be in God's will. God's plan for your life is more about your transformation than your location.

A man walked into a sculptor's studio one day and saw a huge piece of marble. He asked the sculptor what he was going to sculpt out of the marble. The sculptor answered, "A horse." The man asked, "How will you do that?" The sculptor replied, "I'll use a hammer and chisel to take off everything that doesn't look like a horse." In much the same way, God wants to remove everything in our lives that doesn't resemble Jesus Christ. God's plan to conform us into the image of His Son is called by some theologians God's moral will. This is the behavior that He expects from all believers and is universal. God's moral will is found in the principles and commands of Scripture directed to us as believers. For example, in 1 Thessalonians 4:3,7, we read, "It is God's will that you should be sanctified: that you should avoid sexual immorality; that each of you should learn to control his own body in a way that is holy and honorable. ... For God did not call us to be impure, but to live a holy life." We see another example in 1 Thessalonians 5:16–18: "Be joyful always; pray continually; give thanks in all circumstances, for this is God's will for you in Christ Jesus." Remember that God's plan from the beginning has been to make us like Jesus Christ. All of us can know we are fitting into God's plan as we become more like Christ in character and conduct.

What is God's moral will?

God's Plan for My Life Determines How He's Shaped Me for Ministry

Now that we've looked at how we can be part of God's providential will and His moral will, let's look at your life specifically. If you've committed your heart to God's providential and moral plan for your life, God eagerly shows you how He can use your gifts in ministry. In Proverbs 3:5–6 we see the benefit of saying "yes" to God: "Trust in the Lord with all your heart and lean not on your own understanding; in all your ways acknowledge him, and he will make your paths straight." As you allow God to shape your heart and life for ministry, you will see how you fit into His plan for your life. God does the work of a potter, shaping and molding you into a unique instrument for His purposes (2 Tim. 2:20–21). God's been shaping you for ministry,

13

today's session (cont'd)

What is God's personal will?

even before you were born: "We are God's workmanship, created in Christ Jesus to do good works, which God prepared in advance for us to do" (Eph. 2:10). This is what some people call God's personal will.

For example, take the life of Joseph. He experienced betrayal by his brothers, false accusations, wrongful imprisonment, and abandonment in prison for many years. In Genesis 50:20, we finally see how all of those experiences fit together in God's plan: "You intended to harm me, but God intended it for good to accomplish what is now being done, the saving of many lives." Joseph was uniquely shaped to accomplish God's purpose.

Look back over the areas we've studied in this series and look for the common thread God has been weaving in your life. Success is doing what God made you to do!

And take heart from the words God spoke to Joshua just before he took his place in God's plan to give his people a land of their own. "Do not let this Book of the Law depart from your mouth; meditate on it day and night, so that you may be careful to do everything written in it. Then you will be prosperous and successful" (Josh. 1:8).

notes:

Remain in groups of 6–8 people, in a horseshoe configuration.

In this small-group session, students will be applying the lessons of the text to their own lives through the following questions.

The students were asked (in the student book) to choose an answer for each question and explain why.

Learning from the Story (5-7 minutes)

1. Israel waited 70 years for God to bring them back into their land from exile. Which of the following things are you trusting God to do that you've waited a long time for?

   ☐ the salvation of a family member
   ☐ the salvation of a friend or coworker
   ☐ a family member to come back to the Lord
   ☐ to find a job
   ☐ to find a spouse
   ☐ a ministry to invest my heart in
   ☐ other:_____

2. I find the most difficult part of trusting God's plan for my life is that:

   ☐ I have plans of my own.
   ☐ I've been hurt by someone in my past.
   ☐ I am impatient.
   ☐ I am not very disciplined with my time.
   ☐ I am committed to too many things.
   ☐ I don't think God can use someone with a past like mine.
   ☐ Other:_____

3. In which of the following areas does God need to bring you back from "enemy captivity"?

   ☐ my personal Bible study
   ☐ my prayer life
   ☐ my giving
   ☐ my fellowship with other believers
   ☐ my worship
   ☐ my ministry to others
   ☐ my witness to others
   ☐ my thought life
   ☐ my personal relationships
   ☐ other:_____

notes:

13

life change lessons (5-7 minutes)

Share with the class the following thoughts on how the lessons of this text might be applied today. The answers to the student book questions (provided in the margin) are underlined unless the question requires a personal answer.

What are three vital principles from Jeremiah 29:10–14 that help us understand how we fit into God's plan?

God's will is a difficult topic for many Christians. It can seem complex and frustrating. To make it clear and simple, we need to change our approach to understanding how we fit into God's specific plan for our lives. Here are three vital principles from Jeremiah 29:10–14 that we need to remember as we seek to find our place in God's plan:

1. <u>KNOW GOD MORE INTIMATELY BY SCHEDULING A DAILY DEVOTIONAL TIME</u>. Too often we seek God's hand without seeking His heart. In Jeremiah 29:11, we learn that God has a great plan, but His primary focus is that we find Him! In verses 13-14, God says, "You will seek me and find me when you seek me with all your heart. I will be found by you." We must let knowing God more intimately be our deepest desire instead of seeking what He can give us (see Matt. 6:33). When we can't see how the puzzle of our lives is taking shape; when we don't get the answers we're looking for; and when our plans for our lives fall apart, we need to be able to trust in the Lord with all our hearts—and that only happens when we know Him intimately. That's why seeking God for who He is and getting to know Him should be our primary focus.

In reference to following God, what analogy can you draw from the way a shepherd leads his sheep?

2. <u>LISTEN TO GOD'S VOICE BY READING THE BIBLE DAILY</u>. Jeremiah 29:10–14 doesn't tell us to search for His will or plan. Why? Because His plan and will for our lives is not lost; it's in His hands! God says, "I know the plans I have for you" (v. 11). God has called us to be followers, not searchers. God expresses His desire for us to follow Him in verse 12: "Then you will call upon me and come and pray to me, and I will listen to you." In John 10:27 Jesus said, "My sheep listen to my voice; I know them, and they follow me." <u>An interesting fact about sheep is that they can't see well, but they hear extremely well. That is why shepherds lead their sheep primarily by the sound of their voice. Sheep learn their master's voice and follow. We need to do the same. By spending time with God in His Word and in prayer, we can begin to recognize His voice when He speaks</u>. We don't need a microscope or magnifying glass to discern God's plan for our lives. We need a greater ability to recognize His voice.

3. <u>TRUST GOD'S TIMING MORE THAN YOUR OWN</u>. The Israelites had been in exile for 70 years before God brought them back to their homeland. In verse 14 God says, "I will gather you from all the nations and places where I have banished you," declares the Lord, "and will bring you back to the place from which I carried you into exile." Surely during those 70 years some of the people

wondered when or if God would come to their aid. Haven't you wondered the same thing? But God is never late and has never missed an appointment or been stuck in traffic. In Proverbs 16:9 we learn God has a pace in which His plan unfolds and we have a different pace: "In his heart a man <u>plans</u> his course, but the Lord <u>determines</u> his steps." Let's trust God who "in all things ... works for the good of those who love him, who have been called according to his purpose" (Rom. 8:28).

"In his heart a man _____ his course, but the Lord _____ his steps" (Prov. 16:9).

 notes:

  Caring Time   (15-20 minutes)

♦ **CARING TIME**
Remain in groups of 6–8 people, in a horseshoe configuration.

Hand out the Prayer/Praise Report to the entire group. Be sure to allow enough time for the evaluation. If your group is going to continue, also allow time to discuss the covenant on page 151. Close with a corporate prayer.

Pray for the concerns listed on the Prayer/Praise Report, then continue with the evaluation and covenant.

1. Take some time to evaluate the life of your group by using the statements below. Read the first sentence out loud and ask everyone to explain where they would put a dot between the two extremes. When you are finished, go back and give your group an overall grade in the categories of Group Building, Bible Study, and Mission.

 GROUP BUILDING

On celebrating life and having fun together, we were more like a ...
wet blanket · hot tub

On becoming a caring community, we were more like a ...
prickly porcupine · cuddly teddy bear

 BIBLE STUDY

On sharing our spiritual stories, we were more like a ...
shallow pond · spring-fed lake

On digging into Scripture, we were more like a ...
slow-moving snail · voracious anteater

13

Caring Time (cont'd)

 MISSION

On inviting new people into our group, we were more like a ...
barbed-wire fence · wide-open door

On stretching our vision for mission, we were more like an ...
ostrich · eagle

2. What are some specific areas in which you have grown in this course?

- ☐ affirming and encouraging others
- ☐ using my life experiences to help others
- ☐ being mentored and/or mentoring an emerging leader
- ☐ developing a daily quiet time with God
- ☐ finding a way to use my gifts and talents in a ministry
- ☐ developing a habit of studying the truths of the Bible to help me with life change
- ☐ other: _____

A covenant is a promise made to another in the presence of God. Its purpose is to indicate your intention to make yourselves available to one another for the fulfillment of the purposes you share in common. If your group is going to continue, in a spirit of prayer work your way through the following sentences, trying to reach an agreement on each statement pertaining to your ongoing life together. Write out your covenant like a contract, stating your purpose, goals, and the ground rules for your group.

1. The purpose of our group will be:

2. Our goals will be:

3. We will meet on _____ (day of week).

4. We will meet for _____weeks, after which we will decide if we wish to continue as a group.

✝

5. We will meet from _____ to _____ and we will strive to start on time and end on time.

6. We will meet at _____ (place) or we will rotate from house to house.

7. We will agree to the following ground rules for our group (check):

☐ **PRIORITY:** While you are in this course of study, you give the group meetings priority.

☐ **PARTICIPATION:** Everyone is encouraged to participate and no one dominates.

☐ **RESPECT:** Everyone has the right to his or her own opinion, and all questions are encouraged and respected.

☐ **CONFIDENTIALITY:** Anything said in the meeting is never repeated outside the meeting.

☐ **LIFE CHANGE:** We will regularly assess our own life change goals and encourage one another in our pursuit of Christlikeness.

☐ **EMPTY CHAIR:** The group stays open to reaching new people at every meeting.

☐ **CARE AND SUPPORT:** Permission is given to call upon each other at any time, especially in times of crisis. The group will provide care for every member.

☐ **ACCOUNTABILITY:** We agree to let the members of the group hold us accountable to the commitments which each of us make in whatever loving ways we decide upon.

☐ **MISSION:** We will do everything in our power to start a new group.

☐ **MINISTRY:** The group will encourage one another to volunteer and serve in a ministry, and to support missions by giving financially and/or personally serving.

notes:

13

Reference Notes

Use these notes to gain further understanding
of the text as you study on your own.

JEREMIAH 29:10
exile

seventy years. This number marked the beginning of Judah's return from exile (see 2 Chron. 36:20–23; Ps. 90:10; and Isa. 23:15).
bring you back. God would deliver the Israelites out of Babylonian exile (see Jer. 27:22).

JEREMIAH 29:11
God's plan

I know. Although it may have appeared otherwise, God had not forgotten His people. He alone knew what He had planned for His people. This is in contrast to the false prophets mentioned in verses 8–9 who pretended to know God's plan.
and not ... harm. Prosperity and disaster both find their ultimate source in God (see Isa. 45:7).

JEREMIAH 29:12–13

See Deuteronomy 4:29–30. God's gift of prosperity depended on Israel's willingness to turn away from their sins and turn to Him.

JEREMIAH 29:14
return

This is a summary of Deuteronomy 30:3–5.
bring you back to the place. The larger purpose of the exile was to bring Israel back to God (see Deut. 30:3,6–14; 31:23; 32:47; 33:7,26–29; Jer. 30:3; 31:23; 32:36–37; 33:7).

notes:

notes

notes

notes

notes

notes

Name	Phone No.

Prayer/Praise Pages

Pray for ...

Praise God for ...

_____   _____

_____   _____

_____   _____

_____   _____

_____   _____

_____   _____

_____   _____

_____   _____

_____   _____

_____   _____

_____   _____

_____   _____

_____   _____

_____   _____

_____   _____

_____   _____

_____   _____